LEEDS
THE
LOVELY

LEEDS
THE
LOVELY

EVELYN PURVIS EARLE

Foreword by
ARTHUR STRINGER

ILLUSTRATIONS BY IVAN E. SCOTT

THE RYERSON PRESS — TORONTO

Printed in Canada
By The Gananoque Reporter
Gananoque, Ontario

TO

MY FATHER AND MOTHER

IN

LOVING MEMORY

Acknowledgment

The illustrations in this book are by Mr. Ivan Scott, to whom the author extends her special thanks.

I am deeply grateful to the people of Leeds who so kindly loaned pictures and assisted me in collecting folklore during the preparation of this manuscript.

The Origin and Meaning of Place Names in Canada by George Henry Armstrong, M.A., a native of Leeds, was also very helpful. Every reasonable care has been taken to give credit where credit was due. If there are omissions or errors of any kind, the author will greatly appreciate information which will enable her to make the proper revision in the next edition.

If this small effort meets with a favourable reception, the author hopes to write another book about Leeds. Any information which could be used in such a volume will be greatly appreciated.

E. P. E.

Contents

□

I	This Is My County	1
II	Origin and Settlement of Leeds	9
III	Elopements of Leeds	19
IV	Social Life of Leeds	29
V	Lakes of Leeds	41
VI	Houses of Leeds	57
VII	Villages of Leeds	71
VIII	Towns of Leeds	94
IX	Women of Leeds	117
X	Men of Leeds	141
XI	They Return to the Land	160
XII	Journey's End	171

Foreword

☐

To be a pioneer with the pen is as courageous as being a pioneer with the plow. To invade a corner of our country and translate its beauties into language is now as important as the clearing of its forests once seemed. Evelyn Purvis Earle, in writing this volume on *Leeds the Lovely* proves that the Ontarian county that fringes our majestic St. Lawrence, with its clustering small lakes and islands and azure-tinted streams, is a place to be known and loved and understood. She proves, too, that she is a lover of the land of her birth. And that love has given her not only the power to show how our new-world lakeland county of Leeds is no whit less alluring than the old-world Lakes of Killarney, but also to record, with those intimate touches so tied up with affection, the charm of a countryside about which both the native and the visiting tourist has been too inarticulate. Combined with this warm-hearted recording of quaint villages and picturesque characters, of scenic grandeurs and nostalgic memories of a way of life that is passing away, is a transfusing love of the soil and an even deeper love for this Canada of ours. Many others, I hope, will learn to share my delight in this volume.

ARTHUR STRINGER.

I

This Is My County

And the night is tenderly black,
The morning eagerly bright,
For that old, old Spring is blossoming
In the soul and in the sight;
The red-winged blackbird brings
My lost youth back to me,
When I hear in the swale,
From a grey fence rail,
O-ke-lee, o-ke-lee, o-ke-lee!

—ETHELWYN WETHERALD.

I DO NOT REMEMBER a time when I did not know it was lovely, although I can remember a time when I did not know it was Leeds. I thought it lovely when I knew no land but this. Now that I have seen the romantic beauty of Killarney, the wide expanse of Loch Lomond shimmering in the sun of late afternoon, with the castle of the Duke of Montrose, like something out of a fairy tale, on its banks, the Thames under London Bridge and the picture-book land of Bermuda, I still think we have scenery that is unsurpassed right here in the county of Leeds. There is only one place in the world whose beauty, of an entirely different character, gives me such a feeling of ecstasy as the view from the International Bridge or the region around Charleston Lake. That is the long stretch of deep blue ocean reflecting the cloudless sky and the wide white sands at Long Island's Jones' Beach.

I remember March nights when "There was a roaring in the wind all night," and "The rain came heavily and fell in floods." With what drowsy comfort I listened to the strong, fierce staccato of the raindrops beating on the roof! Exulting, I thrilled to the full-voiced volume of the wind, and in that dim consciousness between wakefulness and sleep felt myself borne away on its billows into a region beyond all time and space. Then the awakening in the morning, when the "eagerly bright" sun seemed to have a translucent quality, with pale yellow and blue-violet lights. The tracks of the horses' hooves in the black mud were edged with bluish crystals of ice, and the birds were singing in the distant woods. As it grew warmer, the nights were "tenderly black," with the poignant, earthy smell of the plants coming up in the sweet, warm soil and, later on, the heavenly odours of the wild plum by the picket fence, the blossoms on the gnarled old trees in the rambling orchard and the lilacs by the gate.

WHEN I HEAR IN THE SWALE FROM A GREY FENCE RAIL
OKE-A-LEE, OKE-A-LEE, OKE-A-LEE

Sunday mornings we went walking in the woods, either on our own or a neighbouring farm. Ours was hilly and had mounds which we were told were Indian graves. There were hemlock groves in which we found hepaticas, jacks-in-the-pulpit and wild phlox. There were grand woods on the other farms, where were dog's-tooth violets, blood-root, marsh marigold, honeysuckles, trilliums and many other flowers of Spring. Once on a solitary ramble, I found some tiny white violets with blue centres entirely covering a very small clearing in the woods. And of course the large purple violets grew in a corner of the snake fence.

We lived on a high plain of land, and perhaps that is the reason that I have such vivid memories of the fresh, clean winds of Spring. They are always associated in my mind with snowy white clothes blowing madly on a

line, spotless white aprons on a dark dress and the white
candlewick counterpane on a child's small bed. Rooms
which had been housecleaned were filled with a particularly pleasing fragrance brought by these winds coupled
with the smell of a freshly scrubbed room and a carpet
stretched over tramped-down hay. Moss roses and satin
stripes on the wall paper, old-fashioned maple furniture,
and the frog chorus from the pond haunted by the red-
winged blackbirds that perched on its bordering grey
fence rails made one think with ecstasy of the lines—

> "When on my bed the moonlight falls,
> I know that in that place of rest
> By that broad water of the west,
> There comes a glory on the walls."

The pale yellow moonlight made deep purple shadows
in the room.

It was fun to visit Grandfather's farm in Spring, for
they made lots of maple sugar, tapping over a thousand
trees. They often "sugared off," and the little cakes of
very light maple sugar were better than the candy from
the store. Evenings when there was company jack wax
would be made by pouring hot thick syrup on snow in a
large pan. For supper there would be sponge cake with
thick maple sugar icing, with walnuts spread lavishly on
the top. Here the woods were even more thrilling than
at home; one could walk back to the pond at the end of
the farm, a distance of about two miles. Throughout the
woods one heard the pleasant noise of the waters of
Spring — the little stream bordered with watercress, the
small waterfall with its bank covered with flowers and
the cold spring down below. There was, however, a ser-

pent in this Eden — several of them, in fact — big black snakes five or six feet long, perfectly harmless but terrifying in appearance, that came up from the pond.

Summer was my favourite season. There were so many possibilities for enjoyment in our county. Where other counties may have only one or two bodies of water for camping or picnicking, we have the magnificent St. Lawrence and a host of lakes and smaller rivers besides. Even the people who have always lived here have usually explored only a part of the fascinating lakeland county of Leeds. There is the best of fishing, marvellous and unique scenery and, unlike many other places which have splendid scenery, the summer weather is practically always warm enough for swimming. There is just tang enough in the air to stimulate the appetite and make even the plainest food taste unusually good. Well do I remember a time when we were camping and had run out of food. We had only a sealer of lemonade and a rich devil's food cake left. We rowed up the lake and stopped to eat at Bowsprit, the point where Harter shot his rival, Dockstader, in the famous murder case of over a hundred years ago. To this day I remember it as one of the most delicious meals I ever ate.

But if you really want to enjoy a picnic in Leeds, just prepare it over an open fire in one of the stone fireplaces at Long Lake. This we always found more enjoyable if we had climbed Mr. Towle's Lookout on the high, rocky hill on the opposite shore from the road. From it you can see five lakes. Everything will taste good, but best of all will be steak, boiled corn and maple syrup on apple pie. Make the coffee with water from the lake, and you will be surprised at the improvement in its flavour. A picnic of this kind is especially nice in

October, with the lakes so very blue and the lovely colour of the trees. The view from the Lookout is breath-taking, and it is impossible to describe the beauty of the woods on the shores. Overhead you may see one of the bald-headed eagles who has a nest here or a giant blue heron in awkward flight. It is said that not far from here the largest blue heron rookery in all North America can be found. The lake was closed for some time, and the fish became so tame that they would come up to the shore to eat crumbs from your hand. One plump old bull pout would even let you stroke his head.

Another interesting afternoon may be spent flying over the lake region of Leeds. It is an experience so wonderful that "heavenly" is the only word which is adequate to express the beauty of the county as seen from the air. Imagine a great mass of all the colours of the rainbow, everywhere on it huge blobs of delphinium blue. Everything has an exquisitely moulded, finished appearance. You see no hills, neither do you see any unsightliness from the air. All is neatness and order, the houses so tiny, the farm homes so compact and cosy. The long beige ribbons which are roads with the toy cars on them, the dark green of the water in some places, the blue of far-off lakes, the clusters of houses which are little villages with, as in the case of Morton, a blue thread of water winding through — all this makes you realize that until you have seen it from the air you have not really known Leeds. The Gananoque Airport, now used by so many in Canada and the United States, is only six miles from the Town with the Gates in the heart of the Thousand Islands, and English-born Douglas Wagner, an instructor at this airport in World War II, is one of the best pilots in the land. At modest cost you can enjoy a splendid flight over Leeds.

Winter is a cosy time in this county. Those living south of the border come home for Christmas to century-old stone or brick houses in town or country. There are fragrant logs burning in fireplaces, and silver curls of wood smoke spiralling from large chimneys against a background of snow-covered hills and dark firs into a clear blue sky. Christmas in Leeds is particularly enjoyable in those long-ago settled homesteads with verandah-edged brick or stone houses, deep lawns with cedar hedges and big, well-kept barns. Inside, the spotless rooms are decorated with spruce and hemlock and, in these days of electricity, a lighted tree. A home-grown turkey with potato and onion dressing is roasting in the oven. I once spent a Christmas in an old brick house about twenty miles from town, where they had a small fir tree lighted with brightly coloured bulbs beside the front door. Over the door was an English lantern with a glowing red light. All around were woods and in front of the house a wild, rocky hill, emphasizing the picturesqueness of the scene.

It is perhaps in winter that Leeds is most truly itself. The tourists are gone, although very slowly they are discovering what a fine place it is to skate and ski. Everyone goes mad about hockey. All who can get out on the ice and skate. Almost all the young people, and some not so young, ski. It is a good time for social events. Women's Institutes, Farm and Citizens' Forums have splendid meetings. Adult education classes are held, churches offer most delectable food at their dinners and teas. Much friendly visiting is done. Wild winter evenings can be spent happily beside the fireplace with a book. The stores are not so crowded; it is a comfortable time to shop and have dinner at one of the homelike Victorian hotels which have been serving good food for more than a hundred years.

This, then, is the county of Leeds, a county of snug homesteads, wide, fertile fields, romantic lakes and woods and towns with quiet streets. I had to leave it for several years to learn its worth and appreciate it. I returned from the beauty of other countries with eyes newly opened to the loveliness of the county where I was born.

RED HORSE LIGHTHOUSE, THOUSAND ISLANDS

II

Origin and Settlement of Leeds

Out of the dust God called new nations forth,
The land and sea made ready at His voice.

—MARJORIE PICKTHALL.

THERE WERE GROUPS of hunters and explorers living along the waterfront of Leeds before the American Revolution, Canada having been British since 1763, but during those decades practically no real effort at colonization was made. After being demobilized, many officers and soldiers who had fought for the King made their way to the county and took up land, thus beginning the clearing of a vast area which was all wild, trackless bush. Then, in 1788, from the states of Vermont, Connecticut and New York, came the United Empire Loyalists, the "King's Men," who, as a "Mark of Honour," were given the right to have the letters U.E.L. after their names.

Some were plain, uncultivated people, others were graduates of some of the best colleges in New England and the British Isles.

I stood one summer day in the vast dining hall of Trinity College, Dublin. It looked, and probably was, unchanged, since my great-great-grandfather Weeks ate there when he studied medicine before coming to Vermont. A U. E. Loyalist, he was given a wild and rugged farm at MacIntosh's Mills. There were few patients in that sparsely settled bush, so most of the time he had to farm. But when he went on calls he did so, of course, on horseback, with saddlebags in which to carry instruments and pills. His great-grandchildren were the first of his descendants to go to college and obtain a degree.

Not far away in the wild and wooded country around lovely Temperance Lake, I talked to a farmer, Seymour Burnham, still working hard on the farm where he had lived for over seventy years. "My great-grandfather was a doctor," he said. "He was a U. E. Loyalist who fought for the King.' I wondered why the U. E. Loyalist doctors did not seem to be fortunate in their allotted farms. True, they drew them from lots in a hat. It may be that they, used to towns and cities, were so appalled by the wildness of the bush that they thought one place as good as another and did not, like many, try to trade for a better tract of land.

They probably did not have a very clear idea of the hardships involved in settling in the bush. Often they

THE BLUE MOUNTAIN FROM CHARLESTON LAKE

had a foretaste in the laborious journey from the States to Leeds. Sometimes small children wandered off and were lost. Having received their allotment, the new settlers set out with their rations given them by the government, travelling, of course, on foot. Possessions and small children were carried on their backs. They were fortunate if they obtained a farm near water, for then they had a way of travelling from one part of the county to another. There were not even tracks, only marks on trees to guide them in the bush.

Arriving at their allotted acres, they erected their first homes. These frequently were tents which had been used in the American Revolution. While the women made the temporary homes as comfortable as possible,

and prepared the simple meals, the men began to cut
down trees and erect a rude cabin of logs. They could
find partridges and other game, while berries of many
kinds grew in great abundance.

A few pieces of furniture were sometimes brought
from the old home, but usually all the beds, chairs and
tables were made of poles and split logs, for there were
no boards. At one end of the cabin a fireplace of stones
covered the entire wall.

After cutting down the trees, the settlers sowed oats,
wheat and flax around the stumps, threshing them in a
burned-out hollow log. The women learned how to spin,
if they did not already know. A spinning wheel and loom
were necessities in every home; for the fine, well-made
clothes many had worn when they came soon wore out.
The Indians taught them how to make clothes and shoes
out of skins.

At that time the whole county, and especially the
Blue Mountain, was infested with bears and wolves.
There were, of course, many deer. Now the bears are all
gone, although in my childhood some berry picker was
always reporting, whether truthfully or not, I cannot
say, that he had seen one; but wolf hunts are still
organized in the county about once a year. Driving over
the Lost Bay road, one is quite apt to see a deer. They
are very curious when I drive slowly by, and will invariably turn and gaze for a minute or two before
leaping the fence and dashing off into the woods.

Once, out at the railway crossing between Moortown
and Wilstead, about ten o'clock at night, I saw a small
spotted fawn. Terrified, he darted away and I heard him
frantically struggling with the wire fence. Late one

night on the Caintown road a huge buck leaped across directly in front of my car, just missing the hood.

For many years the pioneer customs of Canada were handed down from generation to generation. Even to this day, many families eat delicious dried corn. In my childhood a favourite winter snack was tasty dried beef. The pioeneer woman used dried berries in the winter, for there were no jars for her preserves. Even a few years ago, families trying to economize would make a substitute for a mattress out of a tick filled with husks from corn.

"The Duke of Windsor, when Prince of Wales, once told me why he thought the people of Canada were not so fond of reading as those in some other countries. He said he thought it was because we were too near to the pioneer stage," said the poet of Abbey Dawn, Wallace Havelock Robb. Well, I cannot see why this should be so. There are sagas in the early history of any county in Ontario to equal those of the ancient Greeks. With a background such as ours, we should not have to depend for inspiration on a foreign scene. We have been too inarticulate about the fascinating past of Canada. Slowly, however, our writers, along with the radio and film, are making us realize that we do not have to go outside our own country to find interesting material for novels.

Quite fittingly, the county was named after a family whose origin was one of romance. The family of Francis Osborne, fifth Duke of Leeds, was descended from a young apprentice of Sir William Hewitt, Edward Osborne, who jumped from London Bridge to save his master's daughter. (How or why she fell in, history does not say; nor does it say whether she fell in a moment of dizziness or in a fit of despair.) However, later they were married. Their descendant, for whom the county was named in

1792, was made Secretary of State for the Home Department of the British Government that same year. It seems a natural sequence that so many descendants of the early settlers have romantic stories of the founders of their county that have been handed down from generation to generation.

Many Anglo-Irish emigrated to Leeds after the Rebellion of 1798. These were Anglican in religion, Conservative in politics and usually gay and buoyant in nature. The women of the household had equal authority in family affairs, even those of finance. It is doubtful if they knew that the rebellion which caused their emigration had as a leader one of their own faith, Lord Edward Fitzgerald, who headed the United Irishmen when they rebelled. Unfortunately, they were apt to think it a struggle between those of differing faith. In this they were encouraged by their rather prejudiced leader, Ogle R. Gowan, the handsome and gifted founder of the Orange Order in Canada, who was bitter on account of the destruction of his lovely home on his Wexford estate, Mount Nebo.

In Ireland those of Celtic Irish descent had thought these new settlers very English. However, the English and Scotch in Leeds thought them very Irish indeed. After about a hundred and forty years of living in the same county, and some intermarrying with the natives of County Wexford, they were physically very similar to those who came out in the years following the famine of 1841 from Tipperary, Kerry and Cork. Side by side, the descendants of those whose families had been at odds in the Rebellion settled and developed their new homes, each feeling with the other a strange tie which impelled them to be the best of neighbours in time of sickness or need. For after all, temperamentally they were much alike, and besides they had come from the same land.

I remember one of these neighbours with the most affectionate amusement. He and I went to the same school. A miniature Jack Oakie, no turkey egg was more freckled than his broad, comical face. I was shy, and he joyfully seized any opportunity to tease. If we played Clap in and Clap out, he would prance in on bare, mud-caked feet and holler, "This is the wan fer me!" as he bounced gaily into the opposite seat.

"Can I walk home with you?" he demanded one summer day, when I was wearing my new turned-up straw sailor hat with streamers of navy blue about a yard long. "Indeed, you can't!" I answered, haughtily, my own small freckled nose high in the air. I did not even look back, and was quite unaware until years later, when the little sister whom I was leading by the hand on that occasion told me, that he had goose-stepped along behind me all the way home hanging on to the long streamers of my new straw hat.

He grew up to be a fine, good-looking, solid citizen type of man. Now he takes a deep interest in art and, the last I heard of him, was going to paint a picture of Dulcemaine Hill beside our crumbling brick school.

The U. E. Loyalist settlers were mostly of English birth, but many of the early pioneers were Scottish, and they gave a splendid and much needed contribution to the colonization of the county. Outwardly they were a rather serious, reserved folk, but they had a deep appreciation of humour and fun. They had usually a meticulous sense of honesty and justice, an aptitude for business, and a profound interest in religious matters, especially in the development of the Presbyterian Church. Often they did not care for their feckless Irish neighbours, although it sometimes happened that their wives were of that extraction. That was no doubt a good thing, for the Scottish people had a settling effect on the more volatile Irish, and the Irish tended to liven up the more sober Scotch. The Scottish settlers were clever and industrious in commerce, and laid the foundations for many industrial enterprises which flourish to this day. In politics they were usually Liberal. The Orange Order had few, if any, adherents from their ranks.

I developed a mild schizophrenic personality from having a set of grandparents of both Scottish and Irish extraction. Part of the time I was very Irish; when visiting the Scottish grandparents I was verra, verra Scotch. At home I was a Conservative; away with the Scottish relatives Liberalism had its charms. Came the time when I was old enough to vote. I was staying with the Scottish side of the clan. For whom should I vote? Dear me, the Conservative candidate was not at all good-looking, but the Liberal was handsome. That settled it. I would vote for the best-looking man. To this decision I adhered until I went home to vote. "Aren't you glad you have a daughter old enough to vote, Papa?" I asked, timidly. Really, it was an occasion, I thought. Surely he was pleased. "No," said my father, briefly and without explanation. The most chivalrous of men, it was all too plain that he considered woman's place was in the home. Suddenly it occurred to me that if I voted for the handsome candidate I would kill my father's vote. Regretfully, I cast my vote for the man with the plain, honest face.

But one day afterward my mother and I walked down to the polls. Neither told until long after how our ballots had been cast. Then we realized that, except for getting some good fresh air, we might just as well have stayed at home. We had cancelled each other's vote.

"Are you Scotch-Irish?" an American once asked. "No, Irish-Scotch," I answered. He laughed. "There's a difference," he said. There is.

HOW TO REACH OUR COUNTY

No county in Ontario is more accessible than Leeds. Its southern boundary is all on the St. Lawrence, so thousands cross the International Bridge at Ivy Lea. The bridge is about thirty-two miles from Watertown and seven miles from Alexandria Bay. When you enter Canada this way, you are on the Scenic Highway which gives a splendid view of the wide St. Lawrence and the heart of the Thousand Islands. Brockville is twenty miles to the east, Gananoque twelve and Kingston thirty miles to the west. These are among the most interesting and historical of Canadian towns. At Kingston ancient Fort Henry, now open to the public, is as quaint and Old World as a castle in a Scottish town. The imposing Royal Military College is Canada's West Point. Until after World War II the cadets wore red-striped blue trousers, bright red coats with brass buttons, and shining "pill boxes" on the side of the head. Only at Fort Henry can the brilliant old-time British uniforms now be seen, worn by the guides who show the visitors the fort.

If you are travelling from Toronto to Montreal, you pass right through Leeds on Highway No. 2. If you have come first to Ottawa, it is a distance of only fifty or seventy miles to the south by a variety of pleasant routes. If you come down to Prescott from Ottawa, turn right on Highway No. 2, and in a few minutes you are in Leeds County. Brockville, the county town, is only fifteen miles away.

So we hope you'll come to Leeds. We think you'll like it here. Having arrived and found a comfortable hostel, stay and see the county. May what I tell you of it make you linger in Leeds!

III

Elopements of Leeds

If ye gae up to yon hill-tap,
Ye'll there see bonny Peggy,
She kens her faither is a laird,
And she forsooth's a leddy   —ROBERT BURNS.

MANY OF THE PEOPLE in the community in which
I was born were descendants of the eloping couples
of Leeds. There are many such stories throughout
the county, but I shall just briefly tell of the romances in
the families I knew when I was very small. I would be
sitting with my feet on the damper of my grandmother's
brightly polished stove, gazing into the flames, while she,
like most people in their seventies, told story after story
of those pioneer days, almost as if talking to herself.

"Tom Deir's mother was a lord's daughter," she would say. "She ran away from Ireland with the hostler. I remember her living in a log house here when we were young."

I asked Mrs. Deir's granddaughter, Katharine Fodey, who had been a Deir, "Is it true that your grandmother eloped from Ireland?"

"Oh, yes," she said, standing very straight, her hair still quite black despite her eighty years. "She had a step-mother she didn't like. They wanted her to marry someone else, but she didn't like him, either. So she said she'd marry the first man who asked her, to get away from it all. My grandfather Deir, one of the hostlers, heard of it and said to himself, 'Maybe I could make a love match with her.' And, being young and handsome, he did."

It was another member of the family who told me the rest of the story. "It was Lord Hollis' daughter who ran away with the hostler," she said. "After they were married they came back and told her parents what they had done. Her father had a high opinion of the young hostler, so he treated them very kindly. 'You cannot,' he told them, 'remain in Ireland because of the difference in faith and rank, but I will help you to emigrate to Canada.' So he gave them a generous sum of money and went down to Dublin to see them off. He never saw his daughter again."

They came to Leeds County, then a trackless bush, and took up land. I remember the son of this couple when he was a very old man with a long black beard. And I remember his children; the girls had blue-grey eyes, black hair and wild-rose skins, and the men were just as

AN ELOPING COUPLE

fine-looking. One of them was never spoken of without the prefix "Handsome" before his name. Indeed, they said when he was dressed up in his fine Prince Albert to go to the county races he was just like the popular idea of a sporting Irish lord. Definitely, farming was not his vocation. Inevitably, he gave it up.

Before her death, the lord's daughter became a convert to her husband's faith. The priest who attended her said that it had seldom been his privilege to meet a woman of such cultivation and charm.

Lady Bridget Graham, of Ireland, was, says her great-granddaughter, dark and plain. (She probably had her great-granddaughter's vivacious Irish charm.) The son of Steacy, the innkeeper, was tall, fair and very handsome. He and Lady Bridget fell in love. They eloped and came to Canada, first settling in Grenville County, then in Leeds. In another chapter I have mentioned the still lovely house built by her son, John Steacy, near Lyn, Few of her descendants are dark but, oddly enough, of those who are, none is plain.

It was one of the prettiest of the brunette descendants who one afternoon was down on her knees scrubbing her kitchen floor. An immaculate housekeeper, this young, motherless girl would not dream of leaving her brothers for a few days unless everything in the big old farm-house was in apple-pie order. It made no difference that she was going to Ottawa the next morning, where she would array herself in a gown with a long train and fasten on her pretty hair the traditional three white ostrich feathers, before proceeding to Rideau Hall to be presented at the Vice-Regal Court. The house must be clean.

She arrived in the city and was met by a clerical brother, who was also going to Rideau Hall. In great excitement and happy anticipation, she dressed. That she looked lovely, I know, for I have seen the picture she had taken of herself in her court dress. She wore no rouge, powder or lipstick, and she did not need any.

It was raining, so she was carefully wrapped up to preserve her satin gown from being soiled when she entered the cab. She had rubbers on her small feet. The cab entered the stately drive of Rideau Hall. They alighted, and were ushered into the great drawing room where their Excellencies, Lord and Lady Minto, received their guests. The young lady made her curtsey gracefully, without stumbling or faltering, as of course the relative who was present feared she might, on the highly polished floor. A charming young attaché whom she met took her through the conservatories and saw that she had an enjoyable time. It was all just too perfect. Except for one thing.

"Really, if I do say so," said the proud older brother, "you made the most graceful curtsey of all."

"Do you know why?" the sister asked, amusement lighting up her face.

"No," said he, puzzled.

"Well,"— and she broke into peals of laughter—"I had my rubbers on all the time. I forgot to take them off," said the great-granddaughter of Lady Bridget Graham.

"My mother ran away from her father's estate in Ireland to marry the gardener," said my grandmother. We were again sitting by the fire. I was about seven or eight and she seventy-odd. I was fond of stories. I listened without saying anything, for I was sure my grandmother would continue the tale. She sat, her hands folded quietly on her carefully starched and ironed apron, with its pretty black and white border lying so neatly on her plain black dress. Sure enough, she went on: "She was only sixteen, and she didn't like boarding school. My father was a very handsome man; he was called the handsomest man in Brockville when he was foreman of the Jones' potash works there. So she fell in love with him and they ran away."

Vaguely, I listened. Like all older people, she told her stories again and again. I did not then, nor for many years later, care who my ancestors were, but once it occurred to me to ask my father, who I suddenly realized must after all be her grandson, "What was my great-grandmother like?"

"She had brown eyes and a large nose," said my big two-fisted parent, the most romantic of red-moustached, curly-haired Irishmen, if the romance concerned anyone else.

"Dear me, what a dismal description!" I thought. "How old was she when you knew her?" I asked. "Ninety," he said. Well, I realized, even Mary Pickford would not be an intriguing figure when she had lived as long as that. Great-grandma had gone through a lot in those ninety years.

Later I asked grandmother a question or two. "What was your mother's name?"

"Jane Griffith," she said. We did not know it then, but a member of one branch of the family was to be the leader of Sinn Fein. "Her father made the Griffith Law."

"Did she never hear from her father and mother?" I asked.

"Oh, no, they completely disowned her for marrying beneath her. My half-brother went over to Ireland when my grandfather died, but not a cent of the property did he get, though he stayed a year. Too much red tape. My uncle was killed steeplechasing. He was the only son."

She added: "My mother managed to bring a maid, old Kitty, and a feather bed with her."

Now how, I wondered, did one manage to elope lugging anything so unwieldy as a feather bed.

I almost forgot the whole story for years. Youth concerns itself little with the dead and gone. But after

I had visited Ireland, I came upon a picture in an old Dublin magazine of the stern gentleman who had been honoured with a title for making the Griffith Law. Well, he could keep grandmother from inheriting any property, but he could not keep her from looking so much like him that there could be little doubt of the relationship. Did he, I wondered, ever grieve for the brown-eyed, curly-haired daughter he had lost when she was only sixteen?

Great-grandmother had six children when her husband died. Very soon she married again, an American this time. She had two more children and lived to a great age.

Her first husband's relatives brought up the first family. There were no schools, so they had a governess. She was not allowed to teach my grandmother, who had to help with the work. Not a bit daunted, she, whose mother was educated in a private school, taught herself to read and write. At the age of fourteen she was taken to her brother's house in the little village of Escott. Here he had built what he called "a commodious stone house." Not so large by present standards, it is still in good repair. A family who came from Ireland live there now.

The young brother — he could not have been more than eighteen — was very strict with his sister. He would not allow her to go to parties, or any neighbourhood jollification, while she was so young. Grandmother wept bitterly, but he would not relent. However, when she was twenty, she met and married the son of an army captain a few miles away.

Later I discovered that the father of my eloping great-grandmother wrote books on Geology, which may be purchased in Ireland to this day.

A Singleton, founder of Singleton's Corners, now Crosby, fought under Wellington in the continental wars, and became a schoolmaster in Dublin upon demobilization. He eloped with a daughter of the Butler family, descendants of the Dukes of Ormond. Many Pierce and Singleton families trace their ancestry to her.

Shane's Corners is named after a family founded by a young coachman who eloped with the daughter of an Irish landowner, a Miss Frizzell. They were of different rank and faith, but they settled down happily in the bush to raise a large family whose descendants still live in Leeds. She was highly educated, and for some time taught a private school.

I had known a delightful Irish lady for more than a quarter of a century, when she told me that she was first cousin once removed of the famous Lord Roberts.

The owner of a popular lake resort, whom I had known for some years, told me that his eloping grandmother was the daughter of Lord Parsons.

The Churchills of Leeds and their cousins, the Moultons, belong to a branch of the family of the famous Winston.

In the early part of the nineteenth century a dashing young Irish lady eloped with the gardener and came to Canada, bringing with her an elegant green velvet riding habit, for she thought she would probably ride a great deal in the new land. McCallum, Jones, Skinner, Birmingham, Kane and Lambert families are descendants in Leeds.

There is an elopement in Editor Scott's family, also, but I do not expect to hear the story until I have known him for at least another twenty years.

There are dozens of these stories handed down from family to family in the county of Leeds. And in many other counties too, of course.

I have told of these romances of which I know because I have been so irritated by certain passages in the history books which are presented as true pictures of pioneer life to our young. In what is practically a chaste whisper, they say, "Many gentlefolk settled in the new country," and give the impression that they remained a race apart. People will always get married, and it was not long before these gentlefolk had intermarried with the sturdier, plainer sort; and it was a good thing for the colonization of the country and for democracy that they did. The democratic process received an impetus from these elopements of Leeds and the effect may be seen in all its developments to this day. Incidentally, in the case of these elopements, members of the family of the young man with whom the girl eloped were often coming out to Canada at the same time. Often these people who had not been considered equals by the families of the eloping daughters have done better financially and achieved more distinction in national life than those who had come from the landed gentry stock. A sturdier breed was needed for the wild new land.

There may have been a few who lived in the early days like the people in the Jalna novels, but they had to live and work like everyone else as time went on. Had groups of families segregated themselves like that in Leeds, no one would have come to help them at their raisings and their bees. They would not have been able to survive. There were dozens of families with the same background as the Whiteoaks, but they had to do the work themselves, inside and in the fields. The greatest luxury they could have would be one hired girl in the house and a couple of hired men on the farm. And yet in many of the homes a tradition of culture and gentle ways of living was brought down through the years, the effect of which may be seen to this day.

All of these stories are of romantic young girls who left wealthy homes to elope with poor but handsome young men. I know of no instance where a wealthy young man eloped with a poor but beautiful girl.

I do not think that the history of these romantic happenings should be forgotten. In another generation the memory of them might be gone. For a Canadian farmer will tell you freely of one great-great-grandfather who was a blacksmith, but of one who was a baronet he will not speak unless he has known you for at least forty years. He would feel it was not quite the thing. And the young folk would only feel that this was a lot of nonsense they had heard the old folk blethering about.

These young settlers had no preparation for the hardships which awaited them, but they met the challenge of the new land with an undaunted courage. With fortitude and unflagging industry, they did their part in helping to colonize this part of our great Province. So that they might be remembered, I have written these stories that I heard in the firelight when I was a child.

IV

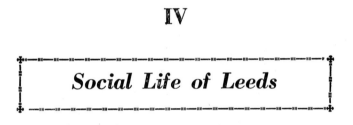

Social Life of Leeds

Oh, the lilt o' the Kerry dancin' !

—Irish Song.

A WAY BACK IN THE 'TWENTIES the young folks might say, with just a touch of superiority, "No, I don't square dance; I can just fox trot and waltz." Now that there is even a Canadian Square Dance Association, there are not many who do not subscribe to this time-honoured and merry institution.

If you want to see the old square dancing in its most carefree and exuberant form, you can find it at one of the local dances in the parish halls of St. Luke's or St. James' in the settlement four miles north of Mallorytown, known as Ballycanoe. Here you will hear the ancient rhymes resounding from the megaphone as that veteran caller-off, Bernard Flood (descendant of a County Wexford family, who have lived on a farm in that parish for many years), calls the changes. As you may suspect from its name, practically all the families in the community are of Irish descent. A musical lilt of which they are quite unconscious will be heard in the soft voices of the light-footed girls.

"I've always loved to dance," said the caller-off, as he paid me the compliment of whirling me around in a lively waltz. "I've been dancing for forty-five years." It was hard to believe, he was still so agile and quick on his feet. But I remembered a picnic in the Toledo woods when I was a child, when we children stood at the edge of the platform, chewing cracker jacks. How the elegant coat tails of Mr. Flood flew in the breeze as he danced happily past with the slender, black-haired, white-skinned girl who later became his wife!

Bennie Leeder is another native of Ballycanoe who is an expert at calling-off. Like the "Billy," by which Mr. W. J. Wilson, of Gananoque, is known, the diminutive denotes not familiarity but affection and respect. On his father's side he is of English extraction, his grandfather belonging to the parish of St. Luke's, he to St. James', but although he is of a usually reflective and studious bent, when it comes to music he is the true Celt. He was born at Ballycanoe and knows a great deal about various aspects of the social life of Leeds. There were, of course, the dances, which they all enjoyed even after putting in a hard day's work on the farm. In winter there was also skating on Graham Lake. Singing school was held in the Sunday School room of the Methodist Church and was

OH, THE LILT OF THE KERRY DANCING

attended by all the young people, regardless of creed. And there were many comfortable homes with snug parlours in Ballycanoe, Caintown and Junetown, where one could spend a happy evening of music and song in the society of pretty young girls.

Young Bennie, however, was different from many of the youth of the day. Although a stalwart, active young fellow, he liked to read, obtaining books from a small library then kept in a Mallorytown home. The books were brought out and returned by the mail carrier. This helped supplement his education. He had had to stop work and help farm while very young, after having had one year of High School. But with his great interest in reading, small wonder that through the years he had sat with benefit to all concerned on the library boards of Brockville and Gananoque, and served in many other important capacities in civic life, while carrying on an insurance business in each town.

He still likes to limber up by taking part in an old-time square, and will still fill in occasionally as a "caller-off." Here are some of the tunes which are used: "The Fiddler's Hornpipe," "Haste to the Wedding," "The Devil's Dream," "Nellie Gray," "The Irish Washerwoman," "Turkey in the Straw" and "Pop Goes The Weasel."

Mr. Leeder tells me the calls are always adapted to the rhythm of the music which is being played. But it is hard to get these gentlemen skilled in the art of calling-off to recite any of the old rhymes. "They just came to me as I went along," says Mr. Leeder. "That's the way with all of us."

"What about the one I used to hear my father repeat?" I said. "The one about 'the girl with the hole in her sock'?"

Mr. Leeder could not remember the rest of that one, but he did finally offer

> First couple lead to the right,
> Be sure you make no blunder;
> Circle four, half around,
> Pop the couple under!

Sounded like a good lively exercise to me. I had probably danced to it without listening to a word.

"What about the one about the birdie?" I asked.

Mr. Leeder chanted:

> First couple lead to the right,
> Circle three, lady inside,
> Birdie fly out, hawkie fly in,
> Hawkie fly out,
> And give birdie a swing,
> And lead to the next—

Mr. Leeder was warming up. He gave me some basic instructions as to the changes, which I had never tried to remember, having always been one of those deplorable square dancers who are propelled along, for the most part cheerfully, by a good partner, and who have an uninhibited desire to step-dance on the corners. Most of us in our extreme youth preferred those lively partners who "knocked the knots out of the floor," hollering "Eee-yeeh!" as they did so.

He quoted some parts I did remember:

> Swing your partner,
> Sashay the floor,
> Once and a half and a half and a half—
> Allemande left,
> Right hand to partner, left to the next,
> Salute when you meet and pass her by,
> And swing when you meet and all promenade.

There is a peculiar swing and lyrical rhythm to the style of the old calling-off that defies description. It has a powerful effect on the dancers, fairly sweeping them into the spirit of the thing in a manner that is almost epic.

A lively square dance is often performed to the tune of "Turkey in the Straw," with the following calls :

> The ladies to the centre and back to the bar,
> Gents to the centre and form a star.
> With right hands crossed say how do you do,
> Left hands back, and how are you?
> Pass your partner by and swing.
> Promenade.

Mr. Leeder often called off for the Mallorytown dances; quite elegant affairs they were in those days. Some of the ladies might even wear long white kid gloves. There was only one intermission, when refreshments were served. He was usually pretty tired at the end of the evening, for he had walked over six miles.

"Dancing was more graceful then," said Mr. Leeder. "The girls wouldn't dance with a man who was the worse for liquor. Only the men drank, and not many of them."

He was paid two dollars for an evening of calling off. The refreshments, however, were always exceptionally good. The caller-off could eat all he liked, and it was "on the house."

The revival of the old square dances is, he thinks, an excellent thing. They are very sociable, and they are good for the health. It is these old-time dances which are really the folk dances of Leeds.

The breakdown was the third change and, as I remember, it always had something rather dramatic about it. Folks were really beginning to let down their hair.

> Honour your partner,
> Honour your corner lady,
> All swing and promenade to place.

I finally persuaded Mr. Leeder to give me the unexpurgated version, which runs something like this:

> Honour your partner,
> Corner salute,
> Swing the girls and go lickety-scoot!

Then the breakdown continues:

> Balance all, all swing,
> Allemande left, right hand to partner, left
>   to next.
> Swing when you meet and balance all,
> Swing and allemande left — to place.
> All swing and balance all. Swing.
> Allemande left. Grand right and left all
>   the way 'round.
> Swing when you meet and promenade to seat.

In this dance no one would be stuck with an un-desired partner. He just danced her right into her seat.

I tried vainly to persuade Mr. Leeder to transpose a few of these calls into what I vaguely remembered as some not too classical lines. He was adamant in sticking to the proper version. But I suspect that, when he is really in action, the influence of an English forebear dis-appears, and he is in his own Celtic element, singing out heartily, "Sw - ing your partners!"

FALL FAIRS

Fall fairs are still one of the big events of the year. Crowds attend the fairs at Lansdowne and at Delta, which have been held for over a hundred years. Fine exhibits of cattle are shown. There are exciting horse races, with the jockeys gay in bright pink, green, yellow and blue satin coats. Children go about eating cracker jacks and big wads of that candy which looks like pink cotton. The latest in household appliances, engines and cars is shown in the fair house and on the grounds.

In my childhood, all the newly married or engaged couples appeared at the fairs as if on parade. It was a little rural Ascot, with the men in derby hats and best suits, the girls in long, pale pink, blue or all white silk frocks. For weeks before, everyone was busy getting some astonishing costume ready for the "Fair." I made my debut at the Lansdowne Fair at the age of four in a flaming red eiderdown coat and white fur-trimmed hood.

Then came a time when no one dressed up. During the war, interest in the fair died down. Men came to the fair in sweaters and an old pair of slacks. Women wore just anything they happened to have. However, of late years the old custom has revived. People are again beginning to dress up for the fair.

Some of the young girls had a lot of fun dressing up one year. They wore lovely old dresses and hats as they helped serve, or just provided atmosphere, to a handicrafts booth. The slender young things looked like pictures out of a *Godey's Ladies' Book,* as they reclined on an old-fashioned love seat, which was part of the mid-Victorian furniture with which the booth had been furnished to imitate a parlour of that era.

It was impossible to keep them in the booth. Out they went among the crowd, swishing their trains and flirting demurely behind their fans, where Herbert Leacock, erstwhile "Blacksmith of Dulcemaine," was waiting, attired in a high silk hat and a swallow-tailed coat. Gaily, this handsome, black-eyed gentleman of eighty rollicking years helped the Victorian belles into a high-wheeled "buggy" with seats facing both ways. Off they went around the track. A thunderous clap resounded from the hundreds on the grandstand when they passed. All around the grounds they went. Occasionally the exuberant Mr. Leacock stood up and, waving his whip, sang amusing Irish ditties quite in the manner of Sean O'Shea when he drives his jaunting car around the Lakes of Killarney on a fine summer day.

Mr. Leacock is a typical Leeds County resident of Irish descent. When I was a child, he was the tall, curly-haired blacksmith of Dulcemaine. The school children liked to stand at the door and watch the bright flames of his forge, or see him shoe a horse. He and his gentle, kindly wife are always remembered with affection for their kindness to the children of Dulcemaine. Childless themselves, their family was the whole school.

A couple of handsome bachelors were strolling about, looking at the exhibits at the fair. One lingered in a booth to examine a small automobile made by Mr. Albert Small, of Gananoque, which really could be driven. Looking up, he saw that his companion had disappeared. He went out into the grounds and was utterly astounded to see him coming toward him, decked out in a silk hat and swallow-tailed coat. He looked like the great-grandfather of both of them, a jolly old army captain who had often come to the fair in just such an outfit, probably in a gig. He, too, was taking his turn in driving the girls around the track. He had been talked into it, he ruefully explained, by a loquacious woman who had ruthlessly exploited his well known good nature.

For the busy housewife of the early part of this century, there was not very much social life, even if she had had the time and strength for their enjoyment after the hard labour which was entailed by the lack of almost all the labour-saving conveniences which the average woman now enjoys. But the coming of the hydro has made a great change. Now the women on the farms, as well as in the towns, have the time to take part in social activities hitherto enjoyed by only a few.

For the women of the village and in the country, the Women's Institute has been of inestimable value for the last fifty years. Perhaps no other person has done so much for the women of this century as the late Adelaide Hoodless, when she formed this remarkable society for all types of women. The Women's Institute numbers among its members women of all creeds and occupations. Not only do they learn useful crafts, knowledge of citizenship and current events, but they put on excellent plays, concerts, socials, dinners and suppers, whose proceeds are used for any worthy cause.

One of these Institutes, the Fairgrove, put on a fashion show at Lansdowne, which was an unusual success. Four hundred came to the supper and show. The versatile ladies of Fairfax and Eden Grove worked hard all afternoon preparing the hall for the event. All morning they had been roasting chicken and other delicacies for the supper. Then, supper served, most of them were transformed into glamorous models for the show.

It was a little different from most shows. There were all sizes, and all ages from seven to three score and ten. Everyone modelled in a way which delighted the crowd. There were many kinds of outfits, from workaday clothes to gorgeous gowns with furs.

There were also men.

The men of Paris who modelled recently had to be carefully assisted on to the stage, so great was their fright. Not so the gentlemen of Leeds. Clad in handsome gabardines and tweeds, they strode manfully out upon the stage with the utmost nonchalance. You would think they had been doing it for years.

They had said of one model, a husky, good-looking farmer of middle age, "He's too bashful; he'll back out."

He and his pretty wife made a fine appearance, first in the attractive working clothes worn by the farmer of today, then in the clothes they wear to church. He had on a well-cut suit of gabardine and a heavy overcoat of a dark tan, of the best of cloth; she was a picture in a beige dress trimmed with brown velvet, shoes to match, and a little off-the-face brown felt hat. As a final touch, she donned a smart brown fur coat.

In a lull between proceedings, everyone was much entertained to see a couple jitterbug madly across in front of the platform in the liveliest manner. We rubbed our eyes, astonished. Could it be ... yes it was ... the bashful farmer, with a gay little Dutch war bride, who in wartime had entertained the troops as an amateur actress in Holland.

A man from Montreal, who was watching the affair, said it was just as good, and more interesting than such doings in that city.

Much credit for the success of the show was given to Marnie Davis, who looked after the wardrobe, and Mary Skinner, the beauty counsellor, who was make-up artist. Both were from Gananoque.

The Radio Farm Forums are doing a great deal to provide social life for all kinds of people, as well as for the promotion of intelligent thought. In town, Citizens' Forums are bringing together people of all creeds and walks of life to learn what is going on in the world, as well as to enjoy a social time.

The Federation of Agriculture and the Junior Farmers are bodies which not only do a great service for the rural people materially, but also provide social events throughout the year.

Social life in town is much the same as in all small towns across the land. There are almost too many affairs to be crowded into one's life. There are, of course, the bridge clubs, the church organizations, badminton, bowling, skating and ski-ing, the hockey matches, bingos, etc., to which nearly everyone goes. In a few centres study clubs have been formed, but bridge is still more popular than Forums with the women of the town.

Cocktail parties are popular among certain groups. Curling and hockey are the absorbing interests of the men during the winter. The service clubs meet weekly and put on formal dances and other affairs.

In the summer there are regattas and motorboat races on the St. Lawrence, at Rideau Ferry, Charleston Village and Newboro. Many of the townsfolk spend the summer in their cottages on the islands in the river.

Some of the farmers have cottages on the river, too. Occasionally one will make his cottage habitable all the year around, and retire to it instead of to town.

For many, picnics are the most enjoyable happenings of the summer. There is a choice of so many lakes such a short distance away. Food tastes so delicious by the water in those interesting woods, and the drives to and from the picnic places have scenery which is unsurpassed. You can travel over various roads to reach these lakes, and all of them are full of charm.

There is definitely plenty of social life in Leeds. The people are never bored, for there is recreation for all.

V

Lakes Of Leeds

There is a magic in this lonely lake,
Star-sown with lilies where its quiet bays
Lap silence from the winds that pause and hush,
Remembering the calm of forest ways.

Dawn breaks its heart in gold upon the wave,
And dies in scarlet stainings whose fire glow
Of cardinal and rose will live again
When the banked fires of memory are low.

But sweetest is the hour when all the lake
Is soft with slumber, and from lilied bay
And sandy coign, singing, the fisher folk
Draw homeward at the dusking of the day.

O magic lake among the lonely hills!
Lost is my heart and wandering in your ways
Of loveliness through lakeland aisles of blue
Lost am I evermore in beauty's maze.

FORTUNATE INDEED IS THE TRAVELLER who
decides to stop for a week or longer in the town of
Gananoque, for he is within a few minutes' drive of
the fascinating lakeland of Leeds. Much of it is lost and
wild and unknown even to those who have lived in the
county for many years.

The region about Charleston, a lake five miles north of the village of Lansdowne, is very much like that of Killarney on a small scale. The scenery is somewhat similar, the numerous islands just as beautiful, and for at least four months of the year it is warm enough to swim. There is a romantic loveliness about the shores and islands, the air has the tang of the north and every mile that you cover as you row up the lake brings vistas as enchanting as a dream. Much of the shore line is rocky and rugged, but here and there the beach is sandy and shallow, the water clear and free from weeds.

On a height of land above Charleston Lake, I began to remember. It has always been difficult to believe that it was not here, instead of the big white house at Warburton, that I was born. The house in which we lived was very small, the only large room was the kitchen; there was a small parlour, a still smaller bedroom just big enough for the enormous bed and washstand of the cumbersome suite then in vogue. The high-topped dresser was in the parlour, outside. The upstairs was not done off at all, and a lean-to held a supply of wood. There were two orchards, one encircling the house and one farther down, just above the caves, where grew the rosy streaked snow apples. The land around the house was only partly cleared, the ground rather bumpy and uneven; here and there were little islands of picturesque trees. Across the field in front of the house were deep woods where the ground dropped down suddenly, forming dark caves in the rock. In them snow might be found in June. My father called the place "Siberia," a very fitting name.

Down below the far orchard were great cracks in the rock. The sandy shore, covered with birch and cedar

SUNSET ON CHARLESTON LAKE

trees, was about sixty feet below. Here and there were caves like small rooms. Dainty ridges of fern grew on the sides of the rocks. In Spring honeysuckle and other bright-hued flowers sprang from the crevices. Later, raspberries and black caps might be found at the top of the caves. The view of the lake was superb; one could see large islands and the Blue Mountain beyond. At the beginning of the caves was an enormous pot-hole where the Indians had ground their corn.

There was only one place where you could go down to the shore, a sort of rugged pass through the rocks. One had to be agile to negotiate it without stumbling and rolling down on to the shore below.

Down under the hill back of the house lived the John Slacks, a U.E. Loyalist family who had first settled near Athens when that region consisted of fifteen miles of unbroken forest. This family had then about a thousand acres of the surrounding land, which they still own, although the big white house with its high verandahs has been vacant for many years. The children of this house were the first playmates I ever had. There were two or three other houses here and there in the woods, but none in sight. High and lonely stood the little grey house on the hill.

My mother did not like living in this wild place. Her home had been a comfortable brick farmhouse, and she had taught school in a thickly settled community. Often she must have been afraid when she would be alone there all day long with a young child. I was only a baby when we moved there on account of my father's health. He recovered his strength in those two years, rowing on the lake every fine morning before breakfast and doing no heavy work. He had rented the home farm. There was plenty of fishing. One could flush a covey of partridges any time while walking through the woods which covered nearly all the two hundred and sixty-seven acres of the rough land.

There were, of course, no conveniences. Soft water was obtained from the rain barrel at the end of the house, drinking water from the pump quite a few rods away. It was five miles to the nearest store.

We had, however, a chestnut horse called Daisy, and a couple of cows. I loved to hear the cow bell on old Whitenose tinkling in the dense woods.

My parents were a young couple in their thirties. They had not a great deal of work to tire them, so naturally there were many evenings when they entertained their friends. On these evenings it would be a homey scene with much laughter and gaiety. The damask and wedding silver gleaming in the glow from the ruby-bowled lamp would brighten the dingy kitchen of the little grey house. Mother presided quietly in a full-skirted

brown dress with quaint puffed sleeves, her lovely face
flushed a delicate pink from preparing the meal. My
father would probably have on his old brown tweed or, if
the company was someone special, a dark suit. But the
most amazing sight, in which he saw nothing amusing
whatever, was that of my father when he was really
dressed up in his best for some special event. Indeed, I
remember well his wearing this particular outfit to
church. It consisted of a very white shirt with a stiff,
glossy front, collar and cuffs, gold or pearl cuff links and
studs, a black broadcloth "swallowtail," as he called his
morning coat, satin striped trousers, shiny black kid
boots, and a brocaded cream satin tie. These were the
clothes he had worn at his wedding. They were good
quality, so he wore them for years, long after they had
gone out of style, when his family had grown larger and
he just couldn't afford another tailored suit. They looked
very well on him, for he was straight and tall, with a
typical Celtic appearance, dark curly hair, grey eyes, red
moustache and sideburns, which he wore about twenty
years after they were outmoded.

In the summer someone was always coming to picnic
or fish. The first fish I ever saw was a large pike caught
by my uncle, a theological student down from Queen's.
Often we had picnics on the islands not far from the
shore. We rowed over in the skiff and spread a white
tablecloth on the warm ground. The lunch might consist
of boiled potatoes and corn on the cob, kept hot in a large
iron pot. There might be fresh or preserved raspberries,
cookies and iced cake. From where we ate, we could see
far up to the "Big Waters" towards Charleston Village at
the other end of the lake.

Often I go back to this height of land and the sandy shore below the caves on Charleston Lake. As with difficulty we climb the hill, which is so rough and long that Daisy had to rest at the bottom, in the middle and at the top, I hold my breath for fear the old Ford will not make the grade. When it has rained it is apt to stick in the mud. At the top Daisy's feet always went "clop-clop" on the flat bare rock. The quarter of a mile from the hill to the site of the grey house leads through dense woods, which are romantically and wildly beautiful and have altered not at all through the years. But when we come into the clearing, all is changed. Gone is the old log barn, gone is the little grey house; only the well remains, partly covered by boards. Only one or two apple trees stand. The little houses over the hill beyond the Narrows, as we called the land above the caves, are gone, too. It is a lonely but still beautiful uninhabited land. Or was, for now several cottages have been built by men who like to go there to hunt and fish on nearby shores. Trucks rumble up the long hill and past the cellar of the old house, where once a dark-haired young woman stood at the door in the lonesome afternoons with a small, plump child clinging to her skirts.

One of the islands of Charleston Lake is larger than the rest. Once it was a hundred-and-twenty-acre farm. It was owned by William Crozier, who lived there with his wife and several sons. There was a comfortable farmhouse, since destroyed by fire, and barns. One winter's night we went across the ice and had supper there, later listening to the boys playing old-time music on the organ and violin. Being about three, I spent the evening sliding up and down the walnut sofa, which was covered with the black horsehair then so much in vogue.

When I explored the Lakes of Killarney, in Ireland, I saw a footman bringing his employers a tray with afternoon tea. They must have brought the materials for making tea with them. You will not see anything like that on a similar type of shore on Charleston Lake, but all along the shore, especially on a holiday or a Sunday, you will see many picnic parties.

The little settlement called the Outlet is at the end of the lake, five miles from Lansdowne Village. Until about twenty years ago, there was only one cottage there, on Greer's Point. Now there are quite a number there and on the opposite shore. There are also cottages along the stream, really a river, which flows out of it, and which is called Wiltse Creek.

There must be at least a hundred and twenty-five cottages on the shores and islands of Charleston Lake. People come here from many parts of Canada and the United States. They come to rest and enjoy the boating in these lovely surroundings and to fish for the noted salmon trout. Charlie Cross, assisted by his two sets of twins, will take parties up the lake to Charleston Village or any other place desired. It is fun to go to Aunt Nell's Hotel and enjoy her delicious pies.

It is a nice outing to go to the Blue Mountain by way of this lake. There are plenty of boats and outboard motors for rent at the Outlet, and in a short time you are on the shore, where the climb to the top begins. If it is midsummer, you can pick huckleberries all the way to the top. The view from the highest point is superb.

On the east side of the mountain is Basin Lake, which may be reached from Junetown, four miles north of Mallorytown. It is perfectly round and very lovely in the autumn, bordered by brightly coloured shrubs and trees. Not far away is another small body of water, Mud Lake, and Mountain Lake, near the top, is also tiny and covered with moss.

A favourite drive of mine is not far from the Outlet. It leads into the yard of the John Slack farm. Instead of taking the turn to Lyndhurst at the Woodvale School, you go straight on until you come to a Y in the road. To the left is the grass-grown track which will take you to the site of the little grey house, to the right is the road to the Slack farm. It is a drive of unusual beauty, but can only be taken in a truck or an old Ford, when the weather is dry. Enchanting glimpses of the lake may be had all along the way. Finally you come to the ruins of a log dwelling, which was the pioneer home of the Slacks.

There is a tragic story of a long-ago happening in this lovely part of the area around the lake. In 1860 two young men, both still in their 'teens, Harter and Dockstader, from Evans Mills, New York, came to hunt and fish. They were cousins, and both were in love with the same girl, who favoured Dockstader, the more personable of the two. Harter, as it turned out, was insanely jealous of his cousin because of the girl's preference for him.

They spent their first night in Canada at the home of my great-great-grandfather, Dr. William Weeks, at MacIntosh's Mills. Then they went on through the bush and spent a night at the old log homestead of the John Slack family, which still stands, although the roof is gone.

On a lovely August morning they started off through the thick, deep woods. They obtained a boat, and just as Dockstader stepped into it, Harter shot him in the back.

Then he wired stones to the head and the feet and dropped the body into the water. It was not, however, very deep at this point, for a ledge extends for some distance from the shore. But further out he might have been seen. Returning, he told everyone that Dockstader had been accidentally drowned.

Now, so far it had all the elements of the perfect crime. But a few weeks later came a dreadful storm. The body was blown in toward shore instead of up toward the Big Waters, as he had expected. Justice was swift. Harter was publicly hanged in Brockville some time in December. Six Americans, probably relatives of Harter, were present with a sleigh. They seized the body as soon as it was cut down and made off at a furious speed across the St. Lawrence. Fearing pursuit, they hid it in a barn under some hay until spring. Then Harter was buried in an old deserted cemetery, for, of course, the body of a murderer could not lie in consecrated ground. For seventy years a monument with an account of the crime carved on it stood over the grave. A few years ago it mysteriously disappeared, and now one with the usual inscription stands in its place.

The crime took place on the Slack estate, at Bowsprit Point, as it was then called. Since then, however, it is usually referred to as Judgment Cove. To this day, there is something sinister and melancholy about the lonesome spot.

If you turn to the left at Woodvale School, you soon come to Killenbach Lake, named after an early pioneer family of Leeds. Two aged residents of the Outlet, picturesque Mrs. "Mary" Watson and her brother, are its only surviving members.

Killenbach is a long, lonely lake with only a white house and a couple of cottages on its banks. The road winds along a lovely shore beside a wide expanse of water. On the left is a high, wooded bank. You make a sudden sharp left turn and begin the ascent of a steep hill. Stop here and climb over the fence, still keeping to the left. A well trodden path leads to a high hill, where from Mr. Towle's Lookout you can see five bodies of water, a most gorgeous view. Long Lake lies at your feet; Charleston, Lost Bay, Killenbach and Higley are limpid patches of blue among the rugged hills. Mr. Towle, a native of England, at one time rector of the Lansdowne parish, used to love to sit here and meditate and smoke his pipe. He was a clever man of a definitely literary turn of mind. Only recently have many Leeds residents become aware of the unusual beauty of this place. Now, almost any fine Sunday when you are driving by Long Lake, you will look up and see figures silhouetted high against the sky on the opposite hill.

Returning to your car, you next come to the tortuous hairpin turns of Gulf Hill. At the bottom of the hill a track leads to Higley, a lonely and beautiful lake which is uninhabited. You can drive along its wild, densely wooded shore for about half a mile, if you have a small truck. There is an old loon of an immense size back there, who bitterly resents any human intrusion of his domain. One day when we saw him, he was skittering madly and happily at an incredible speed over the surface of the water, raising as much spray as a small boat.

A little farther on, at the left, are the high, fir-dotted banks of Long Lake, a long, narrow body of water, with very thick woods on the far shore. You wonder if bears and wolves might not still roam about in this area; of late wolves have been found not far away. Occasionally a wolf hunt is organized.

There are several rough stone fireplaces on this shore above a sandy beach. Usually, there is at least one car parked there and a group of picknickers before a crackling fire. In summer there are raspberries on the bushes in the groves, but it is perhaps nicest in early autumn, with its flaming trees.

About a mile away to the left is the turn to the Lost Bay road. On it a gate at the right opens on to the road leading down to Lost Bay, which has one of the most beautiful beaches in Leeds. There is only one cottage on its shores, a very old log cabin owned by Mr. Roy LaRose.

Continuing on the Lost Bay Road, you soon reach Kelsey's Corners. About three miles west, at the end of the winding road, is another large and lovely lake, called on the map Gananoque, but known to the local residents as Sand Bay Lake. Here again is a region much like that of Killarney. Occasionally, you see the ruin of an old log house. Here and there are comfortable home-steads. The shore is very shallow and sandy; you can wade out for a good distance before there is a sudden drop that is really deep. There is a wide open view, and on the islands and shores are a few cottages. Watching a sunset, as you eat a supper you have prepared on the shore of this lake, is something you will not forget. The scenery is like that of parts of the lake districts of the British Isles.

If, instead of turning toward Lost Bay, you continue on the Lyndhurst Road, you come in a few minutes to the Black Rapids Bridge, which connects the Black Rapids with Red Horse Lake. A narrow road at the right passes a handsome farmhouse and ends at Shawmere, a pleasant resort. Just beyond is the crystal mine. Here a clever miner, Mr. Jack Steele, insisted that there was a mine, even when experts disagreed. He was right, and for several years he has been operating it with much success. He showed me the crystals, which looked like the prisms of the old hanging lamp used when I was a child; they were just as perfectly shaped when they came out of the ground. Some of them were as small as a lead pencil, others as big around as one's arm. It seemed too fantastic that they had lain hidden there all those years.

Red Horse Lake is so called because there is a red horse painted by the Indians on one of the rocks.

After climbing the steep, crooked hill, we come to a thick pine woods and then to Long Point. A little farther on, near the old stone homestead of the Singleton family, are the wide waters of Singleton Lake. There are cottages on either side of the road. One fall day when I went past, a Mr. Wickware, whose people once lived in the vicinity, was remodelling, planning to build a fireplace, I believe.

The village of Lyndhurst is about three miles farther on. It is situated on a very attractive body of water, which would be called a river in any other land; here it is a creek. There is a splendid view from the bridge and from the back of the rectory on the hill.

It is not far from the village to either of the Beverley Lakes, which are so beautiful that I wish I knew them better. They may be seen from the schoolhouse at Short Point.

To reach these lakes, you turn off Highway No. 2 at Lansdowne and drive north. There is a very small one hidden somewhere in the woods of Sand Bay that I have never seen. It is called Lime Lake.

If you drive on to Mallorytown before turning off the highway, you can turn to the left at the Caintown sign and go to Graham Lake at MacIntosh's Mills. Here an enterprising Brockvillian, Mr. William Fortier, has built some of the most beautiful log cabins I have ever seen. They have very large stone fireplaces, picture windows and red doors. At sunset the glow of the reflection from the doors colours the fireplaces a deep red. Connected with this body of water are Temperance and Centre Lakes. On the shores of the former are farm houses, which you see as you drive along the Temperance Lake Road. This road is at the right, just beyond the hill at MacIntosh's Mills.

Lake Eloida is not a very pretty lake, but it has long been the site of a camp ground, where a religious sect hold camp meetings every year. It is just north of Athens village.

Instead of taking Highway No. 2 from Gananoque, you can go on Highway No. 32 down the North Road. Not far from Gananoque airport is a lovely little body of water called South Lake. It has a couple of islands and very high banks. There are delightful cottages on the shores. Here two retired business men, Gordon and Garnet, the Sheppard twins, have a snug cottage where they go to hunt and fish. On the walls are the beautifully coloured wings of several of the many kinds of ducks found in the region of the lake. Farther on is a lovely place owned by Mrs. Troop, of Syracuse. It has pleasantly arranged lawns and flowers and is very cosy inside.

Deer go through here at night, past the Sheppard cottage, knocking down the wall built of stones. The sunset seen from the hills is of indescribable beauty.

When you come to Highway 15, you can take a two mile drive to the right down to Seeley's Bay, which is on the Rideau, or you can detour to the right at Olivet Church and go to Grippen Lake. Here is a wonderful camp for boys and girls, sponsored by various organizations in Leeds, with splendid woods and a thousand feet of sandy beach. There are cottages on the shores and fine farm homes in the surrounding area.

Turning to the right on to Highway 15, you come to the turn to Jones' Falls. After a drive of two miles, you reach this well known resort. These waters are part of the Rideau system.

Farther on, you may turn to the left to the good road, which leads to Chaffey's Locks. This beautiful resort has been adequately described in more than one book by those more familiar with it than I. Here is the place to go, if you want to dress smartly and dine among interesting looking guests at Opinicon Hotel, kept by Mr. Don Jarrett, or at the homey farmhouse of James Simmons, descendant of a very early pioneer. Here Mr. Simmons, accompanied by his little blonde grandson, James VI, once took us for the most delightful ride all around the seven lakes. Both the resorts have cottages which are the last word in modern conveniences, with stone fireplaces, electricity and baths.

Westport is on the Upper Rideau. The view from the little mountain at this small town is superb.

Portland has a picture-book view of the Lower Rideau at the end of a little cross street.

I love them all, these lakes of Leeds. Every summer, exploring them is my chief delight. But my heart turns always to Charleston, near which I was born.

The Greer family lived in the big square house at the Outlet when I was small. This has now been turned into a tourist resort by Samuel Horton. Once, in my father's time, this family had a little steamboat in which they took their friends on cruises up the lake.

For a long time the Outlet was undeveloped, but about two decades ago the late William Vanderburg, a native of the Outlet, who was a man with a vision of what the place might be, and Samuel Horton, saw possibilities in the place. They built the first cottages up on the Point. After Mr. Vanderburg's decease, his widow ably carried on. A few years ago, she sold her store and many of her cottages to Mr. Walter Chant and moved a small house from an island to the Point. **Here** she and her mother, a sprightly lass of nearly ninety years, come in April and stay until November, looking after the property they still possess. "We never had to advertise for tourists," says Mrs. Vanderburg. The sympathetic and kindly personalities of these ladies had much to do with that. Recently, six or seven fine cottages have been built on what has been christened "The Burma Road." This wildly lovely part of the shore is opposite Greer's Point.

The store is pleasantly situated in the front of a large house, right up against a high rock and shaded by many trees. Here in the evenings the neighbors and cottagers gather to buy their supplies, eat ice cream and drink pop and enjoy a chat with the friendly Mr. and Mrs. Chant. Dinny, in his red checked shirt, walks along the curving road. Numerous boats tie up at the dock, where Mr. and Mrs. Crozier look out over the water from their little sundeck, bright with flowers. Nearby, Mary and Wilbert stand and watch the evening scene.

Betty Fodey or Bernard O'Grady drive by on their way to the store. They would look quite at home in Southern Ireland, from which their ancestors came. To those who have been in that country, this region will always seem like the "Little Killarney of Leeds."

VI

Houses of Leeds

I would have our ordinary dwelling houses made to last, and built to be lovely; as rich and full of pleasantness as may be, within and without . . . with such differences as might suit and express each man's character and occupation, and partly his history . . . When we build let us think that we build forever. Let it not be for present delight, and for the present use alone; let it be for such work as our descendants will thank us for, and let us think as we lay stone on stone that a time is to come when these stones will be held sacred because our hands have touched them, and that men will say as they look upon the labour and wrought substance of them. See this our fathers did for us.
—JOHN RUSKIN.

EARLY READERS used in public schools had many pictures of the first houses of the type built in Leeds. Many of these log houses were so small that one wonders how they housed the large families which most of them did. A few, like the unusually large Thompson homestead in Holland, near the village of Escott, are still used as farmhouses and kept in good repair, but the majority which still exist are in ruins. In the pictures in the school reader they look very snug, and one can imagine the joy of the traveller when he arrived at a cabin in a clearing after a long trek through the woods. How good must have been the flavour of roasted venison, the fresh homemade bread, the preserves of dried raspberries and other plain, nourishing foods prepared by the capable housewives in the Canadian bush! It was really extraordinary how these women, often from luxurious or at least comfortable homes, adjusted themselves to the rugged existence. Many of them, too, were mere slips of girls in their 'teens.

As the bush was cleared and farms became more prosperous, a new type of house was built, of which many still stand. This was the roughcast and the roughly plastered or stucco, and they were often structures of pleasing exterior. Such is the old Jones mansion in Brockville, whose present owner, Elmer Johnston, has very wisely kept all the good features of this Georgian house. With its lovely situation overlooking the St. Lawrence, its wide, hospitable verandahs, it is somewhat like a mansion on one of the old plantations of the South.

Another large dwelling of this type is ancient Quorn House, in Gananoque, built by a Mr. Briggs and later occupied by another branch of the Jones family. With its dark red trim contrasting against the white walls, its enormous chimneys and good lines, it might be a house in a quaint old village of any of the British Isles.

The solid farmhouse occupied by Claude Purvis, of Junetown, built over a hundred and thirty years ago by his grandfather, is also of this material.

EARLY PIONEER STONE HOUSE

Hugh Lynch, of County Wexford, was a friend of the Webster family, also from County Wexford. They had Mr. Lynch and his son, Peter, build stone houses for them. The Lynches also erected so many stone houses for other settlers of the county that, if placed side by side, they would extend three-quarters of a mile. These still stand, after enduring the storms of over a hundred years. Simple in design, they have a beauty and dignity that lasts and is peculiarly suitable to the Canadian scene. These men built most of the stone houses in the Lansdowne area, and also in the district between Lansdowne and the town of Gananoque.

We found one of the loveliest stone houses in the country one fine September afternoon. For some reason, I cannot now remember why, we had decided to go to

Lyn, by way of Caintown, north of Mallorytown, and straight on through the Cronk Woods. The woods were indescribably beautiful in the September sunshine, as we drove along the grass-grown track which could scarcely be called a road. There were few houses along the way, But presently, to our surprise, we saw at our left a large Georgian stone house, built high and square with many small-paned windows, and with servants' quarters at the side. There was a deep doorway painted green and white and a beautifully shaped fan-light over the door. The house did not face the road but the side of the lawn, at the edge of which was what had once been a grand drive through the ruined wooden gate posts and the avenue of tall elms which circled around to the front door. The tree-shaded lawn had once been landscaped, and there were still some ornamental shrubs formally arranged. The roof was slightly marred by the addition of a small conservatory, long disused, at the very top. About the place was an air of past grandeur and lost romance.

"Why, I remember that house when I was a little girl," said one of our party. "We used to go to town this way in the sleigh. The place looked so pretty with the snow on the firs."

It must have been beautiful, and what a grand place to spend Christmas! How fortunate were the children who grew up in this remote homestead in the woods! It must have been a rather wild country there when the house was built. How, one wondered, did they ever persuade servants to remain.

No wonder there is a romantic air about the place. It was built by John Steacy, son of the eloping Lady Bridget Graham.

I found another interesting house in this vicinity, but this one is in ruins. It was not so large as the first, but it had evidently been built by a man of means. Scarcely one of the small panes of glass in the windows was whole. Even the stones seemed to be crumbling into the soil.

I stopped the car. "I've got to see the inside of that house," I said. So we went in at a side door, stepping cautiously over a floor of wide boards strewn with pieces of glass. We were in what had been a good-sized living room, well lighted, with deep windows, beautifully panelled beneath the sills and at the sides. On the wood-work was the remains of paint of that bluish green so beloved by the French, and fashionable when the house was built. From the living room a stairway with an attractive balustrade led upstairs. At the right of the stairs a curved arch was filled with double doors, which had probably been added for warmth. They opened into a dining room, which opened, in turn, into a kitchen with many little cupboards in the walls.

From the discoloured walls upstairs paper hung in forlorn strips.

The door was blown so fast by the wind that my sister had to climb out and open it from the outside. We left the house standing like a sad ghost in the November dusk. Had a family of gay young girls once lived in those rooms, we wondered. What a lively square dance might have been held there in the past! We could almost imagine the rustle of crinolines down the deserted stairs.

It was evident to our country-bred eyes why the house had been allowed to fall into ruin. It did not look like the best of soil in the surrounding fields.

Houses are to me like people. I gaze at every one I see with as much interest as I do at the faces of the people in a crowd. I cannot imagine any more enjoyable occupation than to take one of these deserted houses and renovate it so that it is once more a home.

The DeNaut house in Delta was built by Colonel Walter DeNaut in 1860. The main part is of stone with walls two feet thick. The coloured servants lived in the brick annex at the side. One window was about fifteen feet high. During the De Naut régime, this gracious residence was beautifully furnished with mahogany and rosewood. There were four fireplaces and broad stairways and an atmosphere of luxurious comfort in this house situated on a hill in a small village in the fascinating lakeland of Leeds. Sir Charles Tupper and other cabinet ministers were frequent guests. It must have been a fascinating sight to see these distinguished guests drive up with bells jingling to enter the warm, firelit rooms out of the deep cold of a winter's night.

Colonel DeNaut was a grand-nephew of Bishop DeNaut, tenth Roman Catholic Bishop of Quebec, who was eventually canonized. Marin, the first DeNaut, came to Ville Marie, Quebec, from France, in 1621.

The De Naut family has not lived in Delta for many years. A son of the colonel, Dr. J. L. De Naut, of Hamlet, Indiana, has sent me a picture of the house when it was at its loveliest. It must have been one of the finest homes in Leeds. It looked a bit lonely the day I saw it. The fence which enclosed it was gone, and a cow ambled leisurely down the side of the lawn.

There is a stone house on the Scenic Highway, a few miles east of Gananoque, which has a magnificent view of the St. Lawrence. It was built by Charles Gray, of

Kilmarnock, Scotland. Russell Gray, his great-grandson, now lives on the place. Mrs. Charles Gray was an aunt of Canada's most famous Conservative Prime Minister, Sir John A. MacDonald, and it was she who planned this imposing stone house, modelling it on a smaller scale after that of a Scottish peer, Lord Scott. This dwelling, high up over the St. Lawrence, has doors and window sills and the caps of the chimneys all of cut limestone, cut by the convicts of Kingston and hauled twenty long miles over a rough corduroy road by Mr. and Mrs. Gray, in a wagon without springs. Upstairs are two panelled rooms which, before they were divided, formed a long drawing room. The huge fireplace was built of brick. What is left of the house is still one of the largest homes in the countryside, but a good-sized wing has been demolished.

Some time ago, it was announced in a prominent Canadian paper that in a certain bank was twenty cents belonging to the late Sir John A. MacDonald, which could not be claimed because he had no living relatives. They did not know that he has at least forty relatives, nearly all Liberals, in the County of Leeds.

Alma Villa, so called because it was built in 1854, the year in which the Battle of Alma was fought, is a many-roomed Georgian stone house on King Street East in the town of Gananoque. It was built by Daniel Freeman Britton, and its present owner, Mrs. Clark Day, and her late husband, have done all they could to preserve its authentic charm. Its wide halls and verandahs, its french windows and well-landscaped grounds, make it a place which gives atmosphere and background to the town. The interior is equally delightful, with its eight fireplaces with walnut frames, some with large mirrors above them and all in excellent condition. Coloured servants were employed here at the beginning of the century.

If you look across a small grassy enclosure back of the lovely gardens of J. D. Matthew in Gananoque, you will see the back of the stone house which was the old rectory — the whole scene might be one of the Old Land — and it is now quite fittingly occupied by a lady who was born in England, Mrs. J. Round. Inside are delightful fireplaces of the Victorian design.

Brockville has many stone houses dating from early Colonial times. Some of them have beautiful fan doorways and deep windows in the thick walls. They are usually trimmed in spotless white. In summer hollyhocks and old-fashioned flowers brighten the high grey walls.

There is a more modern type of stone house on the Ellisville road. It is of yellow sandstone, with the corners of reddish granite. The doors and windows are set in arches, which give an interesting character to the place. At the back is a view of very blue water, the popular camping resort at Grippen Lake. Built by Mr. Benjamin Dillon, this house is now occupied by Frank Tye.

Beautiful in autumn is the old Willoughby house on the Ellisville road, near Seeley's Bay, of mellow sandstone with coloured ivy covering one side. Its deep lawn is bordered by a fine hedge. There is a lovely countryside all around. Not far away is the little low red house where John Bracken, former Conservative leader, was born.

There are some fine stone houses in the area between Gananoque and Lansdowne, such as those belonging to the Landon family and the McNeely's, at Wilstead, the Warren's and the MacDonald's at Lansdowne. The

Warren house is very high and, when first built many years ago by the Findlay family, the third storey was used for a ballroom.

Several of these stone houses have been renovated without spoiling their good features — the old Legge homestead in Gananoque, now the residence of Lawyer Jack Cliffe; the home of Reginald Scott in Athens, and the old Purvis house at Mallorytown, purchased by Gerald Stevens, former art dealer, of Montreal.

At the edge of the village of Delta is a Hansel and Gretel-like house built of small, flat, irregular stone. Bright, flower-filled window boxes make this little home look very attractive and gay.

Rocklyn, home of the late T. J. Storey, is a pleasant example of a Canadian brick house, solidly built with wide verandahs, terraced lawns, flower-filled gardens and all kinds of trees. "Arthur Stringer wrote a poem about my garden," he once told me with pride. Next door is the beautiful brick residence of Mrs. Haffie MacDonald. This large edifice, with its landscaped grounds and wrought iron fence, is one of the show places of the village.

Nearly all of the villages have these brick houses, which look like places in which the tired heart could find peace.

Among the brick farmhouses there are dozens worthy of mention: the Ellis Foley home in Rockfield, a house which would look well on any city street; the homelike dwelling surrounded by verandahs, which is the former South Lake residence of Harold Dempster, of Gananoque, now occupied by Mr. Hough; and the charming domain of Alex Steacy, at Warburton, on the wide, level height of land just before you come to Charleston Lake.

One of the more attractive brick houses is the former home at South Lake of Dr. Sue Thompson Gould, an unusually successful member of the medical profession now living at Old Greenwich, Connecticut. With pleasant verandahs and large barns, it is truly a place one would like to call home.

Well built frame houses have their own individual charm. A mile from Gananoque is the William Webb farm, whose owner wisely refused to leave the farm where he had lived all his life when the time came when he wished to retire. White, with deep, shady verandahs, this lovely homestead is one of the oldest in Leeds. That the country around is fertile as well as beautiful is shown by the unusually large and handsome red barns. It is the birthplace of popular George Webb, former Progressive Conservative member for Leeds. It is a fitting background for men of the English squire type, which in appearance they are.

The home of Wilfrid Webster, of Greenfield, husband of the poet, the late Gertrude Bowen Webster, is a distinctive white frame farmhouse with wide, low verandahs. It has a picturesque backdrop in the Blue Mountain and is set amidst fine, fertile fields. There are splendid big red barns.

The modernized two-storey home of Lawrence Chisamore is a good example of how attractive a frame house can be when it is designed by people who understand what is beautiful in architectural style. It is white, trimmed with soft blue, and has dormer windows well placed. As it is on the Scenic Highway, it has a fine view.

I especially like a low white bungalow in Lansdowne with shutters and trimming of blue.

I was born in a frame house. Part of it has been standing for nearly a hundred years. Of no particular design or pattern, as the years went by it sprouted out here and there in various odd additions bearing no relation, architecturally speaking, to one another and connected by narrow passages and halls. In some of the rooms were doors with iron latches and small-paned windows, in the newer parts were large panes and knobs. Rooms were on different levels, necessitating inconvenient steps. One whacked one's head frequently on the low ceilings upstairs. There were, when I was growing up, two pantries, a "buttery," a cookhouse, two attics and ten other oddly assorted rooms. There was also a verandah, an orchard in which grew the famous St. Lawrence apples and a picket fence all around. About a third of the house has fallen down, the orchard has vanished, and so has the fence. But it was a fascinatingly ugly place in which to grow up.

Perhaps I loved still more another house, of brick, in which I spent many of my childhood days. It is an early Sunday morning in the month of April. In the big kitchen the sunlight is almost unbearably dazzling in its golden radiance, intensified by the clean yellow of the floor and the low, squatty chairs around the oval walnut table with the fat legs. The little mistress of the house, with her prematurely white hair and fresh pink face, sits in the midst of her family and her guests as serenely and with as much charm and dignity as if, rising at dawn, she had not milked a number of cows before preparing the delicious breakfast which all now are enjoying. Not in a house with several servants would things run as quietly and smoothly as in this household, where most of the work is done by one small, frail pair of hands. She does not speak much, but when she does it is well worth listening to. She loves Dickens, Barrie, Burns, Scott; she is well read. The most modest and unassuming, as well as the quietest, of persons, hers is one of those strong personalities that make their influence felt far beyond the confines of the home.

Later on the young folks will go walking, boys and girls, some at the beginning of a first romance, through the park-like woods along the winding road that leads through the bright spring fields, down the big hill, past the noisy falls, on for more than a mile to the end of the farm. The younger ones will scamper along in the rear of the party to pick water cress or wild flowers in the woods, if it is Spring. They will all be very hungry when they come back from the long walk and ready to do justice to the Sunday dinner before church in the afternoon.

There will be a good old-fashioned Canadian dinner. Maple syrup is served three times a day, for a thousand trees are tapped every year.

Or it might be a summer evening. The work done, the elders rest and talk in quiet tones. The light lingers softly on the low mountain, and the gravel drive looks more red than usual against the green of the grass in the gathering dusk. Tired of play, a small child in a muslin frock sits on the cool stone steps at the front of the house and listens to the music being played in the dim parlour with its gold leaf wall paper, its fine Honiton curtains and its suite of walnut and amber plush. Dreamily, she senses things of unknown beauty as she hears the melodies of Mendelssohn, Beethoven, Schubert and Bach. The fragrance of the roses is almost unbearably sweet. It is growing darker, but still she sits gazing at the elms, shaped like huge seats, at the bottom of the terraced lawn, and the thick clump of cat tails beyond the gate.

When there is a moon, she feels that the sense of beauty is too great to be borne. There comes a feeling of ecstasy so sharp that it has the poignancy of pain.

Houses make me think of company, and company of the suppers in Leeds County homes when I was a child. For a true home must not be just a place to live in; it must also be a place to entertain. These homes were very cosy on winter nights, with hard maple, even curly and bird's-eye maple, burning in the red-hot stoves. The first gave a blue-and-yellowish crimson light, and the second had the loveliest odour. On the white damask cloth was laid the best china and silver; out came the bubble glass salt and pepper shakers, with stand of palest pink, or whatever similar treasure the family used for these events. There would be fluffy mashed potatoes, or they might be golden and scalloped, platters of cold sliced beef, finely chopped cabbage salads with walnuts, chow-chow, sauerkraut, sweet pickles, ketchup, a large bowl of gleaming ruby-red fruit, usually raspberries or cherries, lemon biscuits, jam-jams, jell tarts, one or two kinds of pie, perhaps lemon meringue, chocolate or mince —if apple or pumpkin, it was liberally laced with maple syrup — a huge layer cake with white cocoanut icing, fresh homemade bread and buns, with plenty of strong black tea. Tables were long in those days. Everyone sat down at once, the family, the hired man and the hired girl. Practically everything was on the table when one began to eat. Just to look at the good things was a splendid appetizer, and all that anyone felt was needed.

There was no hurrying over these old-fashioned suppers in those days. Usually it was a long time since they had all met, so there was much to be talked over. There was a great deal of laughter and merriment — how everyone did enjoy those festivities in my childhood in one of the oldest homesteads of Leeds! When we went to supper at other homes, we loved the drive home through a starlit winter night. It made us think of the old song:

On a winter's night,
When hearts are light,
And health is on the wind,
We loose the rein,
And sweep the plain,
And leave our cares behind.

O swift we go,
O'er the wintry snow,
While moonbeams sparkle 'round;
Our hearts keep time
To music's chime,
As merrily on we bound.

With laugh and song,
We glide along
Across the fleeting snow;
With friends beside,
How swift we ride
On the beautiful track below.

O jingle, jingle, jing,
As the sleigh bells ring,
As merrily on we bound.

—Old Sleighing Song.

VII

Villages of Leeds

Sweet Auburn! Loveliest village of the plain.
—OLIVER GOLDSMITH.

T HERE ARE A NUMBER of villages which can be
reached conveniently from Highway No. 2. Of these
I shall always find Lansdowne most interesting, for
a few miles north of this village is the old farm on which
I was born.

It is a village with a rather Irish atmosphere, as it
should be, having been named after Major-General
William Fitzmaurice, Earl of Shelburne, who was created
Marquis of Lansdowne in 1784. The title was probably
taken from Lansdowne Road, Dublin, where he was born.
One of the oldest villages in Leeds, it is situated along a
low hill covered with fine woods. I often wish that

more houses had been built under the shelter of that pleasant slope.

It has one of the oldest fall fairs in Leeds. When we were children, we looked forward all year to the excitement of Lansdowne Fair.

This is a village of comfortable homes and hospitable people. There is a weekly newspaper edited by a tall, dark, dynamic Scotsman, Richard Duff. He and his pleasant and capable helpmeet have taken the town to their hearts, and are vigorously aiding and supporting all such projects as waterworks for the village, sports, a 'teen town, and all kinds of social events. Interesting war brides, such as Mrs. Charles Lynch, of Belgium, and Mrs. George Daly, wife of the village druggist, from Holland, brighten up the local scene.

Since the opening of the Walter B. Reynolds Road, by which in a five-minute drive you can reach the threshold of the International Bridge, Lansdowne stands upon a very interesting future. When the new waterworks are installed, there is no reason why it cannot become one of the most progressive villages in Leeds. Just five miles north of Lansdowne is a large body of water, Charleston, the first of a number of lakes which lend enchantment to the hinterlands of Leeds. The mighty St. Lawrence, indeed, the very heart of the Thousand Islands, is only a few minutes' drive away. Where else can you find a centre where, in such a short time, you can be in one of the most fascinating holiday regions in the world? Undoubtedly, there will soon be tourist places in the village for those who wish to explore the county from a central part of Leeds. As decentralization of industry is becoming increasingly prevalent, manufacturing concerns may be interested in a location in a smaller place. A

THE OLD RIVERSIDE HOUSE IN LYNDHURST

great deal of pleasant democratic social life goes on in this village near the St. Lawrence. Church suppers are especially excellent, you will find.

Ivy Lea is a cluster of summer cottages and tourist resorts near the International Bridge. Here in the heart of the Thousand Islands, the scenery is magnificent indeed. Mount Airy Hotel has a splendid view, as have also the delightful resorts run by the Shipman families. There is a big modern store to which you can drive your car, right down on to the wharf. Luxiurious launches anchor here from some of the big summer homes on nearby islands.

Farther east on the Scenic Highway is Rockport. Here are two summer hotels, Hickory Lodge and Cornwall

House, and a store. High up on a rocky elevation is St. Brendan's Church. Some years ago, a wealthy American told the incumbent that she would be responsible for the expense if he would have this edifice painted white and trimmed with green. He declined the offer. Instead, he had it painted buff trimmed with brown. It looks as if it grew right out of the rock.

There is a lovely wild stretch of country around Rockport. Instead of following the Scenic Highway, you can drive on an almost parallel road through the picturesque woods and across to LaRue's Mills. There a small stream flows into the St. Lawrence, and somewhere in this region may be buried a pot of gold. The legend has persisted for many years.

Inside the fence, as you travel toward Brockville, you see monuments of the flat, table-like kind still found in the British Isles. The largest reads:

HERE LIES THE BODY OF
BILLA LA RUE
BORN AT BATH, ENGLAND, AUG. 7, 1727,
DIED AT HIS HOME UPPER CANADA, AUG. 7, 1817.

William, or, as he was usually called, Billa LaRue, was a U.E. Loyalist of English birth, but of French descent. At LaRue's Mills he built a large frame house, which was a show place in a country where most of the houses were of logs. On the creek he erected a grist mill and built a dam. Here were also rifle pits, which were garrisoned by the British in the War of 1812. After his first wife died he married again, a widow with one child. The marriage was not at all happy, as his second wife had not a pleasant disposition. Long before he died, he was known to be wealthy, and it was said that all his savings were in gold, but that not even his wife knew where they were hidden. He died without divulging the secret. His widow and her daughter spent all the rest of their lives searching for the gold. They dug up the cellar, tore off the oak wainscoting and undermined the great chimney until it fell in ruins. Fortunately, the framework of the house was of solid oak, so it still stood. Then they dug up the garden, and even poor Billa's grave. Not a farthing was ever found. A legend grew up that the house was haunted by the spirit of its former owner, who returned at night to guard the place.

In Thad Leavitt's *History of Leeds and Grenville* is a weird account of several men from the village of Mallorytown who went at midnight, accompanied by a man with a divining rod, to find Billa's pot of gold. They found it and dug, soon striking something which gave forth a metallic sound. Instantly they were surrounded by a herd of small black cattle that chased them away. One wonders if they had been bolstering up their courage in the traditional manner.

"Is the gold still there?" I asked stalwart Kenneth Ferguson, great-great-grandson of Billa LaRue. "Oh, yes, it's still there," he replied. However, he'd never bothered to dig for it.

Mrs. J. H. MacDonald, the former Jennie LaRue, great-great-grandchild of Billa LaRue, was not so sure. "My father didn't think there ever was any gold," she said. She hadn't done any digging, either.

LaRue's widow sold all but a few acres of Billa's huge estate. None of the name now lives in Leeds County. "There may be a few relatives in Michigan," said Mrs. MacDonald. However, the place still looks romantic. I always like to slow the car when I pass by LaRue's Mills.

The entrance to the Young's Resort here has the most beautiful avenue of Lombardy poplars planted, legend has it, long, long ago by the Canadian voyageurs.

Mallorytown, on Highway No. 2, is easily reached from LaRue's Mills. In fact, the highway bisects the place, the newer part of the village being about a block off the main thoroughfare. In this part are several stores with a friendly club-like atmosphere and the delightful old residence of the aunt and the great-aunt of Barbara Ann Scott.

As you proceed east on the highway, you see a very large brick house with a mansard roof, built by the Mallory family, U.E. Loyalists who founded the place. Daniel Mallory and his wife came here from Vermont in 1784. Huldah, the last of that family to live in the house, passed away a few years ago, and it is now owned by George Ruttle. Part of the house has been converted into a unique restaurant and store. Nearby is a consolidated school, and a United Church whose architecture is faintly reminiscent of Queen Anne.

On the way to Brockville are two turns you may take to the village of Lyn. The first runs through the pretty farming district of Yonge Mills; the second reaches the village in about five minutes, but it is a little out of your way. However, the latter is a much better road, and you have a fine view of a deep valley through which runs a little creek.

Lyn was named Coleman's Corners after the founder, Abel Coleman, 1764-1810. In the third quarter of the

nineteenth century, it became an industrial centre in
a small way, and a more suitable name was sought. The
clear stream of water used to drive the wheels of the
mill suggested Lyn. It is derived from the Scottish
"lyne," meaning "a pool, a stream, cascade." It is indeed
right that it should have a Scotch name, for the people
are predominantly of that origin, and, even when they
are not, they seem to have the characteristics of the
Scot. Oh, it cannot be denied that an occasional person of
Irish extraction, such as myself, does creep in, if only on
a visit, but they rarely seem to stay; and if they do, they
soon become as Scottish as heather.

It is the perfect place for a June wedding, this shady
village of Leeds. I like to remember one June afternoon
in the stone church beside the willow pond. We had
driven through the slowly ripening fields between hedges
which resembled those of the British Isles. We were
grateful for the dim, cool interior of the church, with
its rainbow gleams of light from the coloured windows
and the handsome domes lit by electric bulbs. There was
a beam of sunlight on the altar. Everywhere was the
fragrance of flowers.

Surreptitiously, we looked around to see what
Cousin-So-and-So was wearing. We noticed a slender
woman clad smartly in all black, with bowed head, saying
a prayer for the young bride. There was a slight stir of
supressed excitement in the church. The wedding
procession arrived, the pretty bridesmaids in pastel hues,
flowing white satin on the lovely auburn-haired bride.
The minister's Geneva gown was a sombre note against
the bright mass of flowers as he said the age-old words,
which always bring tears to feminine eyes. As usual,
we all thought, there is no prettier place for a wedding

than a stately old village church. Afterward we all went down to the bride's home in a comfortable stone farmhouse, where the most delicious refreshments were served.

"What do you serve at country weddings?" asked a city woman of a country mother.

"Just what you serve in town," was her prompt reply.

From my experience, I would say that this is certainly true.

St. John's Anglican Church on the hill is another fine old edifice. Here in the grass-grown cemetery, Captain Peter Purvis and his wife, Catherine Gardiner, niece of the Colonel Gardiner who was the hero's colonel in Sir Walter Scott's *Waverley,* have slept for more than a hundred years. They are ancestors of Barbara Ann Scott.

Dr. Gordon Richards, world renowned radiologist, was born here, as were also Archdeacon Coleman, of Kingston, and Judge Hawley S. Mott, founder of the Juvenile and Family Courts, of Toronto.

The Cummings family, who had mills here in the early part of the century, lived in the two fine old houses at the eastern entrance to the village. There are more attractive old homes in this village than in almost any other in Leeds. One even has a secret hiding place behind its fireplace and another in the cellar. When it was built, about a hundred and twenty years ago, there were no banks.

On the road from Brockville to Athens is the little hamlet of Forthton, where Highways 29 and 42 meet. I stopped at the store at the front of a house in the village one afternoon. It is owned and run by a descendant of the family who first settled there, John Forth. "I used to know a Gertrude Forth," I said. "Where is she now?" "Oh, she's Mrs. Wheeler," I was told. "She keeps The Wagon Wheel over there." That was the first time I had heard of my old friend coming back from California to run this unusual antique shop in her girlhood home.

A little farther down the Athens road is a very old stone house once owned by Dr. William Booth, a pioneer physician of Leeds. Here he had a ten-bed sanitarium, which has now fallen down. Every day those who were able were taken for a ride in the fresh air by this old-time doctor, who was surprisingly modern in his views.

Just before we get to Athens, we pass Clone House, where another physician, Dr. John G. Giles, M.P.P., lived for many years. He also liked living on a farm while he practised his profession.

For many years this village was called Farmersville; then, perhaps on account of its being an educational centre, with its famous High School and Model School, it was named Athens, as it is still known. Here the first exhibition in the Province of Ontario was held, under the direction of the South Leeds Agricultural Association. Later the fair was moved to Delta, where it is now held.

Athens is a quiet old village with some interesting and well-built homes. The schools are well equipped, and it is keeping its reputation for progress in education by having several classes in adult education. A community centre has been built, and there is a County Home for the Aged. William Roach, father of famous Mazo de la Roche, was once tinsmith here. He attended Athens High School.

"Would you like an Irish evening?" I said to a cousin born in the benighted areas of Kingston, and therefore never having had the slightest chance of taking part in one of these lively events.

"Of course," replied the young Queen's graduate, always agreeable. Besides, she was musical, and so were the people we planned to visit. Another cousin, also a musician, came along, and another of the party had just returned from overseas.

There were folks of all ages in the house in the little village of Toledo when we arrived, having come over from Athens by the back road. There was the plump, short, curly-haired great-grandmother, as full of exuberant nonsense as when she was a girl. There was the blonde grandmother, slender and wide-eyed, looking not a day over thirty-two. There was her blonde daughter with her little son, and a variety of cousins besides.

Presently the music began and feet kept time, but at first no one would dance. The red-haired cousin said he was too old; he appeared quite bowed down by the weight of his forty-odd years. The younger ones evidently wanted to dance, the gay music of the piano and accordion was so tantalizing, but no one wanted to be the first to begin. However, things were entirely too slow for the seventy-six-year-old great-grandmother, a lady straight out of the Georgian age. Seizing one of the younger members of the party, she began to dance madly on her small, still lively Irish feet, her shrewd, handsome face alight with mischief and her naturally curly head bobbing up and down as she whirled around the room. Soon everyone was dancing. Cousin Henry came to life, and we pranced through a hearty square. Tom, on the stairs, made nearly everyone die of laughing as he clowned with his mandolin. Every little while the company would become weak from laughing and dancing and sink breathlessly into their chairs. Then the more Irish of those assembled would undergo a most peculiar change. Their lively and animated countenances took on the aspect of melancholy cows. Then that passed and all was merry again. No one laughed more hilariously or danced more gaily than the bouncing, witty great-grandmother of seventy-six.

It's a friendly place, this little village of Toledo on Highway 29. I remember driving to the village one Christmas Eve, with a full moon coming up in the woods on the left and the sun going down on the wintry fields at the right. That night we walked through those moonlit woods to a Christmas concert in the Town Hall. It was a very lively event, in which the audience was not at all backward in helping to make the show a success. If the interval between numbers was too long, the entire hockey team from an adjoining community rose up and sang, without waiting for the formality of an invitation. If the hero forgot his lines while making love to the feminine lead, "Grab her, Bill!" was the advice shouted to the bashful actor. Others amused themselves by firing peppermints at an inebriated gentleman's bald head, with a fairly accurate aim. The "deacon," as they called him, didn't seem to mind. The young people of this district were unusually good-looking at that time, the men mostly dark and the girls with lovely skins. There is a very old Roman Catholic Church in the village and a United Church which has been standing for years.

Newbliss, not far from Toledo, has a wonderful view of a wide stretch of countryside from the hill above the village.

Addison and Frankville are comfortable little villages between Forthton and Toledo.

South of Athens, you can follow the road to the right until you come to the sign which says "Aunt Nell's Hotel." Turn to the left, and in about three minutes you are in the little settlement of Charleston, on Charleston Lake. As you drive in, you come to the hotel, which has been preserved in its original character for the last hundred and twenty years. When it was first built, it was called after its proprietor, Duffield's Hotel.

This village was settled by U.E. Loyalist families, who probably named it after the old home town of Charlestown, now a part of Boston, or in memory of Sir Henry Clinton's brilliant capture of Charleston, South Carolina, in 1780.

Normally, the village contains about sixty-eight souls, but in the summer the tourists come, mostly from the United States. They love to stay at "Aunt Nell's," the Harbour View Hotel where plump, motherly, grey-haired Aunt Nell, as Mrs. Moulton is known to all her guests, makes everyone feel a part of her big family, and serves delicious pies and cakes, to say nothing of more substantial food. The bar has been turned into bedrooms, and all that remains of its furnishings are the Irish prints, "Going to Donnybrook Fair" and "Returning from Donnybrook Fair," on the living room walls. There is a good-sized colony of summer cottages at Charleston, and one American has even built a large house. The fishing is good and the scenery superb. In the evening, bronzed fishermen mill happily about the lobby of the homey old hotel. It is a lovely trip down the lake to the Outlet, a distance of nine miles.

If you come back to the main road, you can drive on through Oak Leaf and, turning to the right, be in the fascinating village of Delta in a very short time. This village on Highway 42 was once called Stevenstown, after Elder Abel Stevens, who was granted a patent to 700 acres in 1796. Stevens was later ordained a Baptist minister, and in 1811 founded a church that was shared by the Church of England until 1864. The land for the church was donated by Nicholas Mattice. William Jones built a mill in 1808, and in 1812, Nicholas Mattice built the present mill, and the name of the village was changed to Stone Mills. Walter DeNaut bought the mill in 1859. Later the village was called Beverley, after Sir John Beverley Robinson, Chief Justice of Upper Canada, who presented the bell to the lovely church begun in 1811 and completed after the war of 1812-1814. The present name, was adopted about 1866, no one knows why.

Upper and Lower Beverley Lakes are connected by Mill Creek; it might be called a small river in another land. The village is situated half way between the lakes. The Upper Beverley was once a small stream wandering through a long, deep valley. When the mill was erected the waters were dammed back, flooding the valley. The stone bridge succeeded one of timber, and this bridge became the dividing line between the reds and the blues, the north and the south, who fought it out in open election style often with clubs and fists. The Beverley Riots took place in this historic spot, and were part of the general unrest which came to a head with the Rebellion under William Lyon Mackenzie.

The village was at one time a sort of industrial centre boasting a tannery, the first foundry in Leeds for the manufacture of farm implements (established in

1821), cheese factory, marble works, lumber and shingle mill, brickyard and carriage works. It also was the home of one of the early poets of Canada, Frederick Wright, an M.A. of Trinity College, Dublin. He lived in great want down a lane, sent many poems to The Brockville Recorder, and issued two books of verse, one with the date line, "Beverley, 1855," and another with the date line, "Delta, 1864." A grandson became a member of the Canadian House of Commons from Winnipeg.

Delta has a great deal of character and unusual charm. On the right, as you enter the village, is a cream-coloured stucco Anglican church, which has been in use a hundred and forty years. The green of the ivy is beautiful against the ancient walls. The quaint old street winds around unexpected corners. There are many solid houses of brick and stone. On a back street is the DeNaut mansion, already described in this book. There are schools, three churches and a nicely built town hall. Down on the high, wooded shore there are cottages on either side of the road. Some are quite pretentious, others are small. All are delightful places to spend the summer days.

Annually, a most remarkable fall fair has been held here for over a hundred years. On some days more than three thousand attend. The exhibits are unusually good. Some of the most beautiful needlework in Ontario may be seen at this fair.

Dr. Lorne Pierce, publisher and author and editor of The Ryerson Press, was born here.

On the way to Philipsville on Highway 42 there is a cold spring where everyone stops to drink. It is a pretty place, and the water is excellent. The water-worn cliff above it is a reminder of the great sea that washed these lands before the ice age.

Philipsville itself has nice churches and schools. The old United Church is well built and imposing; the Roman Catholic Church of mellowed sandstone is pleasantly situated on a hill.

South of Delta is Lyndhurst, where the first iron smelter in Upper Canada was erected about the year 1800. Because of this and other local mining activities, it was at first called Furnace Falls. In 1850 there was a carding and fulling mill, a saw mill, grist mill, post office and one small tavern. Okill Jones, who at this time had secured all the water rights, had the name changed to Lyndhurst by the Postmaster General, in honour of John Singleton Copley, Baron Lyndhurst.

Singletons, by the way, are old settlers of this district. There is a family of that name living in a gracious stone house at Long Point, with precious antiques and a walnut panelled parlour.

There are many pretty views of the water from the hundred-years-old bridge with its quaint stone walls, so strongly built by master craftsmen from the British Isles. One can picnic in the little park. Back of the Anglican rectory are beautiful pine groves, and in this delightful place is the summer camp, Hyanto, of the Anglican Diocese of Ontario, used by the Youth and other organizations. It is one of the most perfectely kept camps I have ever seen, and there will be a fine beach when the two enthusiastic clergymen who have undertaken the task have finished cleaning it up.

Not far away is a good place to picnic on the bank of Lyndhurst Creek, above the pleated rocks. There are fascinating drives in all directions in the surrounding district.

It was Maytime, and the world was full of the bubbling gaiety of Spring as we drove down Highway No. 2 one bright afternoon. The waters of the Gananoque River were a vivid hyacinth against the primrose tints of the opening buds on the overhanging trees. Turning right on Highway 15, we soon came to the village of Morton, once called Whitefish Falls, a small community right out of a picture book, set among the rugged hills of Leeds.

I had heard ecstatic praise of this district from artist Ivan Scott. He was born here, and remembers when the old mill did a rushing business grinding wheat into flour. In those days farmers grew their own wheat, and periodically, the "grist" was brought to the mill. No Leeds County farmer's wife at that time was ever short of flour. It had a sort of fragrance about it, the old mill by the Morton Creek, the clean antiseptic odour of freshly ground flour. The miller would be powdered with white from head to foot. Even his eyelashes and moustache were covered with flour. It must have been a rather pleasant way of making a living, much cleaner than farming or working in a factory in town.

Now only a remnant of the old mill remains. All around is some of the most beautiful scenery in Leeds. A track runs along beside the creek and takes you from the highway to the mill. High banks rise from the left of the track and from the opposite shore. There are cedars among the rocks, and their scent, mingled with that of damp ferns and moss, has that freshness which proximity to clear, gurgling water always gives. Under the bridge the stream narrows but broadens out into a small lake beyond the mill. We walked on to the dam, wondering that no cottages had been built in this gorge which in

Scotland would have been called a glen. Then we found one, on the small lake, just about big enough for Tom Thumb.

On the other side of the highway is the brick school which was attended by Ivan Scott. It is unusual, being octagonal in shape. Situated high on a steep hill overlooking the creek, it would make a perfect studio for an artist. It has not been used for many years.

On another hill is the United Church, of white frame, formerly the Presbyterian. There are a couple of stores and on a side street, a quaint town hall.

At the time of the Fenian raids a blockhouse was erected on Sugar Loaf Island nearby. It has, unfortunately, been torn down.

The lot on which the village of Morton now stands was originally granted from the Crown to Josiah Bullard free of charge, June 26th, 1811. Soon afterwards he sold it to Carrey Hoskins. It changed hands several times prior to 1853, when it was purchased from Peter Scholfield by George Morton and Andrew McKee. The settlement was then known as Whitefish Falls. George Morton, after whom it was named, purchased it in 1856. He married Mary, daughter of Senator Christie, who lived in what is now the Senator Hardy residence, and at one time had a beautiful home near Brockville. After his marriage he lived in Kingston and hired men to look after his many interests in Morton. He manufactured the brick used for his large store and other buildings, including the octagonal school, which was called the "Pimple."

Just beyond the village we took the winding road to the left through a hilly, wooded country, and in a few minutes were in Jones' Falls. The large hotel, Kenny

House, in the family for generations, was not yet open, and the store drowsed in the sun. The falls was fretting noisily as its snowy billows tumbled down the side of a steep shore. The century-old locks were constructed by the British when the Rideau Canal was built and are a monument to their skill. One can drive all around, even up to the top of a high hill which commands a marvellous view.

When I was a child, every young girl around hoped to be asked by some young man to drive to Jones' Falls for a picnic on the Twenty-fourth of May. Earnestly she prayed that the weather would be warm, for it was the custom to wear, if possible, a new white dress. I doubt if the girl of today in shorts and sweater looks any prettier than the girl of yesterday in her starched white frock. It was a dainty outfit, even though it was not so suitable to the wilds of Leeds. Many were the engagements announced after the Twenty-fourth. Whether the white dress had anything to do with it, I do not know. I was bitterly disappointed to find that they had gone out of style by the time I was celebrating the Twenty-fourth of May.

Morton Park, just east of Jones' Falls, is a pleasant spot to eat a picnic lunch. Although there is not a body of water near, the pine trees give a cool shade, and there are fireplaces and other conveniences.

Elgin is the next village, and I think it is now one of the most progressive villages in Leeds. Indeed, it shows signs of fast growing into a town. On the right, as you enter, is a large Roman Catholic Church. On a grassy slope farther down is a lovely little Anglican Church. A United Church of pleasing architectural design is on a side street. There is a town hall, a frame

High School and a Public School of brick. As yet there
is no rash of cheap modern houses. There are houses
which are solidly built in the Victorian or Edwardian
manner, set well back in shady lawns on the pleasant
streets. Their numerous stores have an unusual variety
of goods. One can even find English china, ginghams and
other merchandise you do not expect to see.

Both these villages are so pretty and situated so near
beautiful bodies of water that you wonder why each has
not a larger summer hotel. But, of course, Chaffey's
Locks and Jones' Falls are not far away. A characteristic
of the surrounding country is the numerous high, rounded
hills with dark firs set picturesquely against their
undulating sides. One such hill back of Morton has a
wild grandeur accentuated in early Spring.

You can reach Chaffey's Locks by turning off at
Elgin, or by the new road off Highway 15. It has been
described by Miss Mary Ainslie in *Waterways To Explore,*
and by Clint Fleming, who wrote *The Fish Are Rising.*

Crosby, at the junction of Highways 42 and 15, was
once called Singleton's Corners. Egerton Ryerson
Young was born there. He was a famous missionary,
and wrote over a dozen books. From one of these Jack
London took the story of a famous dog and made it into
a best seller, *The Call of the Wild.* When the poor
missionary reminded Jack that the dog and the story
were his, Jack nonchalantly replied, "Of course. You
gather the data, and we authors turn it into literature."

This corner has a wayside restaurant which serves
the best hamburgers and coffee to be found. Occasional
films are shown in an ancient stone building, and there is
one house of lovely yellow sandstone, built in pioneer
times and cleverly preserved in its original tasteful

design. Near here is one of the largest brick farmhouses in Leeds, set high on a tree-covered hill. Indeed, this particular part of Leeds has some of the finest of Canadian farm homes. They have wide, comfortable verandahs and thick cedar hedges.

There are so many good views of Newboro Lake and of the canal at Newboro that one feels it would be pleasant to stay for a week and explore the islands and bays.

In the late summer evenings, long lines of boats home from fishing pass through the locks. In them are American sportsmen and their guides returning to their cottages on islands nearby. It is very quiet and very beautiful at this time of day, with the shadows creeping gradually over the water. The cottages glimpsed on the far islands have a look of romance in a background which has remained for years unchanged.

The Ontario House and Sterling Lodge provide good accommodations for guests, and there are many cottages.

The stone Anglican Church is more than a hundred years old. Near woods which form a fine backdrop to the village is the large Georgian stone dwelling once used as a rectory, now occupied by Mr. and Mrs. Oscar Henne. It looks like an English country house. There is a queer old roughcast and stone building fallen into disrepair, which was evidently an early village school. Low and long and interesting, it looks as if it could be made into a unique tea room by some original soul.

There are modern stores and filling stations; many houses have unusual doorways. One house of stucco has a very high peaked roof, gingerbread trim, a wide green-railed verandah, and a long bridge reaching across a sort of moat, probably an old cellar. In summer this house is surrounded with all kinds of bright flowers. Another high brick house has a verandah at the top of a long flight of stairs, the whole dwelling having a pointed effect against a tree-clad hill.

Driving home, we realized anew the beauty of our county in the very early Spring. The greens of the foliage were so vivid yet tender, the waters a soft, violet blue. A gorgeous sunset flamed over South Lake. The mellow, golden light reflected over the fields gave them a radiance which seemed not of this world.

On our next jaunt we continued on Highway 42 to Westport. A miniature mountain overlooks the village and the Upper Rideau Lake. The view is as fine as many that are famed all over the world. Here on this mountain was built from logs the first Roman Catholic Church of the community. The parishioners had to reach it through the bush, and, although there is now a road along the mountain, the place still is rather wild. It is, however, a lovely spot to roast weiners or corn and have a delicious lunch, looking down on the little town and the blue water of the lake. High above the roof tops soars the steeple of St. Edward's Church, built in 1859. This edifice is so beautifully constructed that it might be a church in the British Isles. It is at the top of a long, sloping lawn; the grounds are very large. That it was erected is due to the efforts of Father F. Foley; contributions were made by those of many different creeds. It is easily one of the most beautiful churches in this Province.

Almost all the houses in Westport must have an excellent view of the water. Some of the buildings have a great deal of charm, especially those on each side of the bridge leading to the top of the mountain. The one on the left appears to be built on two levels in a very unusual manner.

The attractive Tweedsmuir Hotel serves many guests.

A few miles away, north-east of Crosby is another pretty village on Highway 15. It was named in honour of William Henry Cavendish Bentinck, third Duke of Portland. Situated on a hill, one gets an entrancing picture of woods and water at the end of every street leading down to the Lower Rideau. There are several stores, as well as places where one can have a hasty snack, or sandwiches and tea. Green Shingles, nearby, is a lovely place to stay. There are drives that can be taken through the surrounding countryside, where you will see beautiful lakes and woods, and quaint homesteads which have weathered the gales of a hundred years.

Portland-on-the-Rideau, as it is often called, is definitely one of the prettiest villages in Leeds.

Lombardy is another attractive little village on Highway 15, which I wish I knew better; but I regret to say that I have only passed through it. Jasper is another village I look forward to exploring.

Rideau Ferry is a small but lovely resort on the Rideau near Lombardy on Highway 15. Here is the Rideau Ferry Inn, which gives excellent accommodation, and here the annual Regatta draws many thousands each year. The Merrywood Home for Crippled Children, which is sponsored by the Rotarians, is situated at this resort.

It is a delightful journey from Rideau Ferry to the old town of Perth, just outside the boundary of Leeds, on the Tay. You can, of course, come home by way of Smith's Falls.

One of the nice things about Newboro, Westport, Portland and other villages in Leeds is that none of them is a great distance from Ottawa, our capital city, and the fact that all the roads are good is another.

All the counties of Ontario have interesting villages; but the presence of so many lovely bodies of water gives unusual charm to those of Leeds. Also there is something piquant in seeing such solid brick and stone houses, with an appearance of past grandeur, in the villages of the still rather wild woodlands of our county.

VIII

Towns of Leeds

Fair beside the broad old river
Lie the towns as in a dream;
And the heavy-laden barges
Travel slowly down the stream.

ANON.

GANANOQUE — the name falls on the ear as
sweetly and softly as the running of water over
stones, which the word is supposed to mean. It is
on the mighty St. Lawrence; it is bisected by the winding
stream which is known as the Gananoque River. I can
see the St. Lawrence from my back door and the Gananoque River from my front room. As you pass along
the western part of King Street, views of the River St.

Lawrence are seen as if in a frame at the end of the
short side streets, lined by quaint old houses of brick and
stone. Many of the houses have seen a century or more.
Some have lovely fireplaces of marble, or walnut with
porcelain tiles. Back of them are unsuspected gardens
fragrant with roses, heliotrope, lilacs, peonies and many
other flowers which perfume the river breeze.

My first memory of Gananoque begins when I was
about four. I heard my mother talking in low tones to
another woman about some dolls they had seen down the
street; but, being a firm believer in the Christmas Saint,
I did not for a long time connect it with the big bisque doll
in a wicker carriage which I found at the bottom of the
stairs on Christmas morning when, my heart racing
madly, I pattered excitedly down the cold, uncarpeted
steps in my bare feet. As I remember Gananoque in
those days, it was a paradise for children when they
began to wonder what they would find in the stockings
which they hung up on Christmas Eve. I was spoiled.
Sometimes I had a stocking and a tree. But at that time
I was an only child. I remember a window completely
filled with the loveliest dolls, with blonde or brunette
wigs and frilled white dresses trimmed with ribbons of
pink or blue. Gay tops of shining red or green in shades
of a loveliness never again seen sparkled in the windows;
there were brightly coloured tin horns and drums.
Indescribably delicious were the candy roosters of white
and pink, which looked like milk glass, and the red or
amber animals which resembled clear glass. There were
jacks-in-the-box, Noah's arks, music boxes and mechani-
cal toys that went when wound up, the acquisition of
which would make us fairly swoon with delight. I suppose
the children of today have toys which seem just as
fascinating to them, but I cannot think they can be half

as beautiful as they were at that time. Most of them still came from Germany then.

We came to Gananoque in those days in an old double buggy, or a box sleigh. Both were red, the double buggy faded almost to a raspberry shade. One day, when we had travelled into town in the shabby red double buggy, a friend called to my father, "Why don't you buy a car?" "We're spending our money on education instead," replied my father, who had had to stay home to plough when he had completed the First Form work in the Public School, which corresponds to the first year in High School today, at the age of twelve.

Exciting it was when we passed through Wilstead to catch the first glimpse of the river beyond green fields which stretched down to a high, rocky shore. In the winter we had hot bricks at our feet, as we sat bundled in thick plush robes. Until our family was too large, we would have a hot dinner at the old Shiel's hotel. It had a small parlour with a huge black grand piano, and it was redolent of stale cigars. In the summer we turned into a lane, just before we reached town, and had a picnic dinner neatly laid out on a white damask cloth. Men didn't go to town unless they were "dressed up" in those days. Father would be wearing brown tweed or a tailored blue serge suit.

The next romantic memory I have of Gananoque was the year when, looking at least three years older than my rather tender years, I went up to try my Entrance examinations held in the old High School. Mother, being busy with three small children, had in a moment of weakness allowed me to choose my own hat. It had a hard, stiff brim of white straw, and a thick bed of lilies of the valley sprouted up all around the crown. It did nothing whatever for eyes which a candid classmate had assured me were just like saucers, and a freckled nose. Dimly, I realized that something was wrong; but the days when one bought things because they harmonized with one's appearance, and not just because they were pretty, were far away. I still thought it a very stylish hat, although vaguely aware that it might not be quite the thing for a little girl not yet in her 'teens.

I had a wonderful time, as did the other three who also tried from our school. One of them, the wife of the present Principal of the Ottawa Normal School, was only eleven years old. None of us had ever been very often out of our native Dulcemaine. So we went to the movies in a funny little old movie house every night. We were simply enraptured with what we saw. My eyes were glued to the screen the minute I entered the door; I had to be pursued by the usher and relieved of my ticket. Sinking into my seat, I rapturously watched the romances of big, billowy ladies whose outlines I, being scrawny, much admired. Glamorous heroes appeared in stiff straw hats.

When we were not at the movies, we were at the icecream parlours. What looked to us like perfectly beautiful girls, wearing filmy dresses and accompanied by handsome young men, floated in. To us it was all incredibly romantic on those soft summer nights. These were the last years of the days before the "Great War," when people really "dressed up." With their passing we lost something, but of course we gained much in health and freedom when we arrived at the days of dungarees and shorts.

I had been given a huge sum — $1.50 — to spend. I spent it all, too, in three days, eating icecream, going to the movies and treating my companions. I stayed in a commonplace house, about half the size of my own rambling home, but I thought it wonderful. There were no doors with iron latches, small-paned windows, and ceilings that bumped your head. I even thought the view of a large factory was more interesting for a change than that of the wide home fields.

In spite of being out every evening, we all passed. Due to a good teacher, I came first in the Gananoque district.

A few years passed, and I taught in Gananoque for a year, another girl and I being the "baby" teachers on the staff of the town school. "That child doesn't look as though she knew enough to teach school," remarked a gentleman one day, looking critically after me as I passed, big and blonde and bashful, along the main street. He was right. I didn't, but the Board never found it out. As far as I know, I might have been trundling down to the old school yet, if I had not decided to make a change. Somehow I was saved from that fate. I suffered agonies from shyness. I was a bit plump and tall, and I had a pink face. Horrible young men began to recite tables as I passed. One howled out with unappreciated enthusiasm, "Gee, I'm going back to school!" And I thinking I was so dignified and grown up! About myself, I had no sense of humour whatever.

Then I became a trained nurse and passed through the town about once a year. It always looked rather lovely and Old-World after New York. Also, about once a year I dreamed that I was living in a town called Gananoque, although in my dream the only resemblance of the town to the reality was that it was on a river like the St. Lawrence. And always I was so happy to be living in the place. I had first dreamed that I was living there when I was about twelve years old. But of all the towns on earth, it then seemed the least likely that I should live in that particular town. New York City, instead of the Island, perhaps, or even Dublin, but Gananoque, never. But a sequence of unexpected events brought me here in the year 1943. Here I am, and here I intend to stay. After all, my folks have been in this county for a hundred and seventy-five years. I should feel at home.

Gananoque may be, as some say Ireland is, a state of mind. Either you love it or you hate it, but however you feel about it you usually stay. Somehow the loveliness of the old town fascinates one and keeps one here almost against his will. Gananoque has many moods. In summer it is a gay tourist town. Americans and people from other Provinces flock about the streets buying fine woollens and china, whose quality is unsurpassed. You find them happily fingering Scotch tweeds, or deciding on a particular pattern of Spode. Sir Ernest MacMillan and Lady MacMillan come to town; Barbara Ann Scott appears at one of the noted eating places for lunch; George Fulford, Liberal member for Leeds, breezes through the streets. All day long, excursion boats cruise up and down the river. A plane takes passengers for a flight over the Thousand Islands, from the Gananoque Airport or from the dock. Yachts come in and lie shining and expensive looking in the warm sun. Bronzed people climb out and go up town to shop. One doesn't need to go to Paris to see the styles. Just by looking out of your window, you can see fashions from all over the world. Blinkbonnie, the Golden Apple, the Gananoque Inn, the Provincial, and other not quite so old eating places are serving delicious meals to swarms of guests. At Blinkbonnie guests are strolling about or having tea in the beautiful grounds. At the Golden Apple the garden is gay with coloured umbrellas, under which people are eating.

Gananoque is noted as a tourist town. Three people have been outstanding in their efforts and accomplishments toward making it so. First is Mr. W. J. Wilson, the gentleman with the flaming red tie who is well known in Canada and the United States. He has publicized Gananoque and its welcoming gates far and wide. Then Miss Rebecca Edwards, a former High School teacher, also a native of the town, opened Blinkbonnie as a guest house, which featured good Canadian cooking against a background of Victorian charm. It is, as will be remembered by some Gananoquians, the former residence of W. S. MacDonald. Then a clever American, Mrs. Catherine Runyon, opened up the famous Golden Apple, consisting of an old stone dwelling which was the Joel Parmenter place, a frame house where the first Presbyterian minister in Canada, Dr. William Smart, died, and a large grey frame and brick house, now called "The Appletree House," which was the old Brough homestead. Like Blinkbonnie, it has modern conveniences, but has retained its authentic Canadian background.

A good number of Gananoquians spend the summer in their cottages on the shores of the river or on one of the Thousand Islands. It enables the housewife to have some rest and gain health and strength in the sun and air.

In the winter the town returns to its character of a very conservative and, in some ways, old-fashioned Canadian town. Bridge clubs flourish. Church organizations hold social events of various kinds. Study groups meet and hold vigorous discussions. Nearly everyone is interested in hockey. Many spend evenings at the beautiful Public Library in the park. On the wild nights of winter, when the wind sweeps across the river, it is pleasant to snuggle up to a blazing fire in one of the cosy old fireplaces with an interesting book.

Saturdays the town is full of rather well dressed farmers with their wives and families. They are glad to have such a fine place to shop. Even yet it is doubtful, however, if we know just how lucky we are. Americans realize that here you get woollens for much less — and of far better quality — than you can in New York. As for china, it is unsurpassed outside the British Isles.

As the town is in the heart of a lake district, in the fall there are many parties shooting deer and wild ducks. In fact, it's a fine time to visit Gananoque in the autumn. The scenery along the river and around the lakes must be seen to be described. Motoring is pleasant at this time of year. More and more, other tourists than those who hunt are visiting Canada in the autumn. It may well be that touring Canada at this season may become very popular. If so, there is not a lovelier place in which to ramble about than our countryside, when the woods are aflame with colour and the lakes as blue as the clear, cool skies.

Recently Gananoque has built a large modern High School, which has made the students hate to leave when they graduate. Indeed, there is a rumour that one young chap just refuses to study enough to pass, because he is so delighted with the beautiful and well equipped High School! Probably just a rumour, but it shows how the place is appreciated.

There is a warm glowing heart in the town of Gananoque. It is the Public Library situated in the Town Hall, a solid brick edifice which was the gracious home of Charles MacDonald. It was built, say the records, about a hundred and ten years ago; but many of its features on a larger scale are the same as those in the home of Captain Cartmer, of Cluny Hall, a house three miles from Kingston which sheltered Sir John A. Mac-Donald when he was a child, and which was erected in 1812. It has much the same type of fanlight, leaded irregular panes of a fancy shape beside the door, and the stair rail is of the same design. One wonders if the same architect was employed for both houses. Whoever he was, he certainly knew how to build a dwelling which would stand the ravages of time and retain its beauty throughout the years.

The library is on the second floor, the municipal offices and the Council chamber are on the first. In the Council chamber is a painting of Colonel Joel Stone, the founder of the town, and very aristocratic he looks with his powdered hair and the lace at his wrists.

Every evening a steady stream of people pours in and out of the brilliantly lit Town Hall. Often there are more men than women, for the men of Gananoque are reading as much or even more than the women. The librarians, Mrs. George Whaley and Mrs. Ida Sargent, who are delightful hostesses as well as custodians of books, are in part responsible for the increasing popularity of the place. They create a homey, comfortable atmosphere, and are always willing to give valuable advice as to what you should read. Mrs. Whaley, breezy and jolly, makes much merriment and cheer, the quieter Mrs. Sargent, with her soothing presence, puts everyone at his ease. A very efficient Library Board has worked hard to make the library one of the best to be found in any small town. Mr. B. F. Leeder, who had been for many years on the Board of the Brockville Public Library, has been partly instrumental in the opening of a reference room which is of great value to the town.

The Town Hall stands in a lovely little park. There is a baseball diamond at the back and a bandstand in front. Concerts are held here in the tourist season. The grounds are shaded by enormous trees. There is an appropriate war memorial and many small white crosses in memory of the fallen on the grounds.

In the golden light of early Spring, after an April rain, the trees and the old red-brick mansion silhouetted against the sky have a breath-taking beauty that one never forgets.

You must know the people before you can really know the town. Mr. W. J. (Billy) Wilson is one of the citizens who give colour to the local scene. Nearly everyone calls him "Billy," but the diminutive denotes, not familiarity, but rather affection and respect.

He was born at Wilstead, and it was probably from his family that this community three miles east of Gananoque got its name. That he is partly of Highland Scotch extraction is evident when you look at this strong-jawed, black-eyed gentleman. It would not take much imagination to visualize him as having worn a kilt. Although his formal education did not extend beyond that obtained at the local school, he has accomplished more than many with years of academic training.

He always wears a crimson tie, the brighter, the better, for he loves red. His scarf is usually of the same shade. They suit his personality. Lately he carries a cane, with a handle of bright red.

During his early youth his father, Hugh Wilson, sold farm machinery down at the farm. Then they opened up a business on the main street of this town, selling also organs and pianos for many years. Early in life he married Portia McArthur, a girl with hair of a beautiful auburn shade whose duplicate I have never seen. Her encouragement and help meant much in his career. They have no children, but Mr. Wilson has in a way been godfather to the town. He it was who had the gates built at the east and west of the town and compiled the slogan, *"Gananoque, the friendly town where the gates are always open."* Ever since, it has been known as the Town with the Gates.

For fourteen years he was mayor of the town. He has, without remuneration, operated a tourist bureau for many years. He has held many important offices in tourist associations. In his work he is assisted by quiet, capable Mary Funnell.

"King Edward?" inquired a taxi driver, as Mr. Wilson hopped off a Toronto train. "No, just Billy Wilson of Gananoque," said the blithe Mr. Wilson, enjoying his own informal title, as well he may. He has travelled a great deal in Canada and the United States, and everywhere, by speeches and pamphlets, he has made people conscious of the beauty of the region of the Thousand Islands and of the Rideau Lakes. It is chiefly due to his efforts that our town is so famous as a summer resort. People confide in him and ask his advice, sometimes, it is rumoured, even about love affairs (but that I cannot confirm). He is one of the best known as well as one of the most interesting personalities of Leeds.

Mrs. Ernest Chisamore is a lady who has never lost her zest for life. She writes the Wilstead chronicle of happenings, takes part in church and other organizations, and, after years of farming, went into the tourist business on her own farm at Chisamore's Point, where she has a number of cottages. Her life also is another proof that the latter decades can be lived with enjoyment. She also comes of a very old pioneer family of Leeds.

Another Gananoquian I would have you meet is J. D. Matthew. This tall, slender, white-haired gentleman always reminds me of a colonel of the deep South, even to the slight accent acquired during years of residence in New Mexico.

At the back of his house are beautiful terraced gardens, the terraces being connected by stairs. Everywhere flowers riot in masses of colour, there are all kinds of vegetables and berries and a small greenhouse in the centre. The roses are unusually lovely. The view might be that of a corner in the British Isles.

Mr. and Mrs. Matthew are deeply interested in the Horticultural Society, and it is partly due to this interest that so many dingy spots have been made beautiful. With such a pleasant hobby as gardening and with a great love of reading, this couple find much that is of interest in their quiet lives. The house is of red brick, sweetly mellowed by time. It is the kind of home that reaches out welcoming arms, that grandchildren love to visit, and think of with longing when far away. It is one of the nicest "home" places of Leeds.

Mr. J. Bulloch, formerly of the firm of Parmenter and Bulloch, is of Scottish extraction. In his possession is a figure of Napoleon, beautifully done in brass by his grandfather.

In his earlier years Mr. Bulloch had two hobbies, horses and boats. Now in the years of his retirement he has another — clocks. Some time ago he became interested in their repair and, although he is utterly self-taught, he has yet to find a clock in need of repair which he cannot make as good as new.

When you enter the house you hear the ticking, like a huge swarm of bees. Big clocks, grandfather or Empire style, little clocks, cuckoo, Little Ben, Steeple clocks, French clocks, and clocks of no particular design, all restored to their original condition. One morning about one-thirty, Mr. Bulloch came out of his study with his face simply radiant. "See this," he said to his wife. In his hand was a piece of metal so thin that it looked like the gossamer wing of a butterfly. After hours of effort, he had made this delicate part which was necessary for the repair of one of the clocks. He is an artist in this line of work.

Mr. Bulloch, a great reader, would like to have known Charles Dickens. I am sure Charles Dickens would like to have known him.

Mrs. Bulloch, the former Edith Drummond, was of the Drummond family associated with early Canadian banking and the building of the Rideau Canal. Always of a literary turn of mind, she was often hostess to Pauline Johnson, and had in her possession a brooch which was made for her by the poet's father, G. H. M. Johnson (Onwanonsychon), Head Chief of the Six Nations Indians.

Mr. Frank Eames, who lives on an island near Gananoque, is a native of Chichester, England. He has done, and still does, much interesting work. Not only has he written several brochures, including one about Gananoque, but he also writes poetry, which he illustrates with sketches of exceptional merit. All this he has done while employed in a factory, or caring for the island home belonging to a New York family. This versatile gentleman is a musician of considerable talent. "We are eighty, but our fingers are not arthritic," he announced, as he played a spirited selection on the banjo for me over the telephone. And, indeed, they were not. He has a most interesting library and a hobby for collecting rare books. One of these books is a volume of the poetry of Frederick Wright, who was born in Delta. He finds the study of history fascinating, especially local lore. Altogether a rugged, sprightly gentleman who has come to most pleasant terms with what should be — but for him is not — old age.

No one, except perhaps Mr. W. J. Wilson, has had a greater influence on the town than Harry Campbell, who has been in charge of a Junior Boys' Club for over twenty years. Every Saturday they meet in the lecture hall of St. Andrew's Church. Useful lessons in deportment, kindness to animals, and many other things are taught. There is always a speaker, and no member of a service club can introduce him any better than one of Mr. Campbell's boys. These boys are of all creeds and racial extractions. There is no recreational director in the town, so it is fortunate that anyone so devoted to the interests of the boys as Mr. Campbell does this work— without remuneration.

Gerald Woodley is the present mayor of Gananoque (succeeding Don Carmichael, whose life story is another Horatio Alger tale). The first was William Byers, father of Dr. J. R. Byers, former head of the T.B. Sanitarium at St. Agathe. Dr. Byers, a scholarly and well informed gentleman, who knows a great deal about the early history of the town, now lives in Gananoque. He paints excellent pictures of Leeds County scenes.

Another of Gananoque's eating places which has a distinctive background as well as good food, is the Provincial Hotel, built by Mr. Cheevers in 1859. He sold it to Cornelius (Neil) McCarney, who was the oldest man in the hotel business in Canada when he died at the age of ninety-two, and probably no one has ever exceeded his record of being in that business for sixty-seven years. His son, Harold, assisted by his son, Neil, now operates the hotel, Neil being the third generation to welcome guests at the Provincial. Gracious, unassuming Mrs. Harold McCarney makes the place seem like home.

Jack McCarney, nephew of Harold, is the proprietor of the quaint and beautifully situated Gananoque Inn, which grew out of a factory, the old Canada Carriage Works. Now it is a large, rambling place with an Old World look, where you can obtain delicious food.

One of the most fascinating buildings in Gananoque is the pump house on Kate Street, in charge of Mr. and Mrs. James Stevenson. It is of red brick covered with ivy, with enormous arched windows and a fanlight over the door. There is a wide view of the river and the yachts and other craft which cruise up and down all summer long. Part of the pump house is one of the nicest dwellings in the town. With its extremely high ceilings and lovely furniture of solid mahogany, walnut and rosewood, it has an air of mellow charm belonging to a more spacious age. Even the ceilings of the pump room are beautifully decorated, and the woodwork is excellent. It is warm in winter and pleasantly cool in summer.

Altogether, a delightful place to live. Summer visitors love to explore the place.

Another meaning for Gananoque is "A Place of Health." No one exemplifies this more than Severe Dorey, who will be one hundred and six his next birthday, which is in July. He can read without glasses; he can still walk down street for a chat with his friends and a glass of beer. The Dorey family, of French extraction, once owned the land where the Federal Parliament Buildings now stand.

But probably the most accurate translation of Gananoque is that given by Frank Eames in his monograph, *Gananoque: The Name and Its Origin.* After intensive research, he came to the conclusion that Gananoque means "entrance or way to the mountain." As the Indians obtained flint from a mine in the Blue Mountain region, this may very well be the correct version.

BROCKVILLE

I was about ten years old, but I had never been on a train. With a heart beating high with excitement, I sat in the Lansdowne waiting room, marvelling that the folks around us could look so placid. For we were going on the train to Brockville, to the Fair! Of that exciting journey I remember little, except that we passed the pretty waters of Escott Pond, long since drained; but the Fair was all that I had wished. A wonderful lady in tights walked along a wire on a ball, there was a big, shiny red automobile, and I ate cracker-jacks for the first time. Paris, I was sure, could offer nothing more.

Two or three years went by. I had passed the Entrance but had stayed at home for some time afterward, as I was adjudged, quite rightly, too young to go

away to school. Finally, it was decided that I should
attend the Collegiate at Brockville, so preparations were
made for me to go. Not too many new clothes were
bought; many I had were not worn out, and, being of
good quality, were considered good enough to wear to
school. Among them was a set of Persian lamb fur, of
the best fur obtainable at the time. To this day I
shudder when I think how I suffered, wearing that loath-
some affair, which went around my neck and hung down
in front, and was called by my grandmother a "tippet."
The gauntlets, lined with black velvet, were as huge as
the gloves of prizefighters; a high fur cap was tilted
above an indignant freckled nose. Not once did it occur
to me to refuse to wear them, for in those days we really
did believe that mothers knew best. However, great was
my joy when a young aunt, sensing my discomfiture,
made me the present of a blue felt hat in what was then
the latest style.

Brockville seemed to me such a vast place after the
wilds of my native Dulcemaine that I could not imagine
how my smartly dressed cousin, horribly embarrassed by
my gaucheries, had ever learned to find her way around.
I was continually losing my way and having to be shoved
back into the proper route. I was much impressed by
everything that I saw — the stately churches, the houses
with big-paned windows, instead of the tiny ones in many
of the windows of our sprawling old house at home. Our
home actually had iron latches on a few of its doors, and
the ceilings upstairs were so low that one was always
bumping one's head. I was annoyed because no one
carried a book bag such as I had used at Public School.
It was so uncomfortable to carry a dozen books on cold
mornings. They became wet when it rained and were
always falling out of my icy hands.

But I loved the old town. One autumn evening my aunt and I took a walk down to the fabulous "East End." How beautiful the old mansions looked in the twilight! Leaves were burning with a spicy fragrance blended with the scent of the river back of the houses. What, I wondered, must the life be like that was lived there, so different from the fresh, free existince on a wide old Ontario farm.

Military parades fascinated me. When the Twenty-fourth came, we joyfully dashed out to see the marching Forty-first, with our kind Principal as captain, at its head. Sometimes on Sundays they went to St. Peter's Church. We invariably went, too. Unfortunately, no one had told us to observe the beauty of its architecture. It was not a part of our education then.

But I think I loved the town best on the early mornings of Spring, when pale yellow and purple lights glinted on the broad river. As I walked to school, I saw the water framed like a picture at the end of each intersecting street. The solid houses of brick and stone accentuated the loveliness of the view. No modern monstrosities had as yet made their appearance, and I am thankful to say that Brockville's beautiful dwellings are still kept much as they were. Fine Georgian doorways with fanlights are still spotlessly white, and the old-style verandahs kept in repair. Ivy covers the ancient stone walls.

We urchins from the country had a rather thin time. As I have said before, our clothes were not so smart; we were quite dreadfully out of it with the fashionably dressed town crowd controlling the social life of the school. There was no doubt a rather wry social justice in this. Most of us came from folks who had had their turn at dominating the social scene of the county not long before.

I am always glad, however, that my social life at that time was practically non-existent. It gave me a chance to get a great deal out of the studies I loved — English, the languages, history and art. In mathematics I would never accomplish more than a pass, and chemistry and physics were to me a dreary waste of time. Our teachers were a strongly individualistic group, who left a deep imprint on our lives. They were the last of an era in which education was regarded as something to enrich one's life, and not merely a preparation for a position to earn a living.

There were times when, no matter how unexciting the usual round, one thrilled at being part of the old school. Times when on Field Day we tore around with streamers of red and black, the school colours, attached to our coats, or when, gathered in the assembly room, we were taught to sing by Mr. Key, a handsome and portly English gentleman. Somehow, he taught us in such a way that the dullest was impressed with a sense of beauty and romance. Often we sang:

Oh, hush thee, my baby, thy sire was a knight,
Thy mother a lady, both lovely and bright . . .

or, in warlike vein:

Men of Harlech, cease from slumber . . .

Thrills tingled down our spines when we sang liltingly:

By Killarney's lakes and fells,
Emerald isles and winding bays . . .

or:

In the gypsy's life you re-e-e-ad
The life which all would like to le-e-e-ad . . .

THE GANANOQUE RIVER FROM THE SWING BRIDGE

Perhaps it was just as well for us more imaginative children that the world of reality was so bare and empty. It left time for the growth of a sense of perspective, and for the mellowing effect of thought and experience that can hardly be found in this more hectic age.

It was in Brockville that I saw "The Bohemian Girl," my first grand opera. A group of girls in their 'teens and twenties, among whom was an aunt, decided to see the performance in the part of the old opera house which was then known as the "Gods" or "Nigger Heaven." But, laughable as it is to recall, we did not go without a

chaperone. We had with us a much older lady impeccably
arrayed in well cut black-and-white kid gloves. Audible
remarks about "the poor ladies" floated toward our
embarrassed ears. But how we enjoyed the singing of
the full-blown, bosomy ladies and the husky gentlemen of
the cast!

Often on Saturdays we went to the 'Burg, as we called
the sprawling little city of Ogdensburg on the other side
of the river. To us the dresses and suits found in those
shops were out of this world, so much did they surpass
our home products in style. With what rapture, at the
age of fourteen, did I pick out a pale blue summer dress
with a wide pleated skirt, and later a brown tweed suit
with a velvet collar! Customs officials did, of course,
exist, but they were kind, easy-going souls then.

The trip to the 'Burg was very fascinating as we
drifted slowly down the river on one of the steamboats
which were in operation at that time. And there was a
faint aura of undefined wickedness, of what character we,
in our innocence, could not even surmise, about the little
American city. We had never heard of the French duke's
mistress who had once lived there and whose residence is
now, I think, a museum; but the belief that there was
something iniquitous about the place gave it a subtle
allure. One day, greatly venturing, two of us boarded a
street car and went all the way around the belt line. Many
years after, I drove my car all about the town and tried
vainly to recapture the old spell.

One of the most interesting places in Brockville is
the Eastern Ontario Hospital, down at the eastern
approach to the town. The buildings are old and impressive, of a fine brick red, and there are magnificent
grounds. A relative held an official position in this

institution, so some of us occasionally went skating on
the rink, or dancing with the more rational in the spacious
ballroom.   One of our partners, who used to bow us
through the Lancers in a most courtly manner, was a
former lawyer.   He was always immaculately dressed and
had a red rose in his buttonhole.

I wonder now if there were more Easter lilies at
that season then.   It seemed as if the lovely fragrance
were everywhere.   And always, one certain afternoon, it
would suddenly be really Spring, the snow would be almost
gone, and streams trickling in the gutters glittered
brightly in the sunlight.   Coloured flowers appeared on
Easter hats, and the air had that electric, vibrating
freshness which heralds that happy time.

Like Gananoque, Brockville has the best of English
china and British woollens in the shops.   There are also
smart dresses and well tailored suits for men or women.
One can have good meals in pleasant surroundings at
various places.   Some of the hotels are very old and have
about them the aroma of a more leisurely age.

Brockville was once called Snarlingtown, because of
the dissensions among its citizens; but there is no evi-
dence today that such tendencies have been handed down.
As two prominent families had the right to have the
town named after them, Sir Isaac Brock wisely settled
the dispute by calling it after himself.   The name seems
peculiarly suited to the character of the place.

Captain Peter Purvis, the first of my people to
come to Canada, settled on land now occupied by the
Brockville Cemetery, in 1776.   Later he moved to Yonge
Mills, acquiring seventeen hundred acres in that vicinity.
My eloping great-grandmother, sixteen at the time of her

marriage, and her husband, who became foreman of Honourable Charles Jones' Potash Works, lived in a house situated just back of Victoria Hall about 1828. Their children, including my paternal grandmother, were among the first babies christened in St. Peter's Anglican Church.

Some day I hope a history will be written of this lovely old town. All I have attempted to do is to describe it in relation to myself. Colonel F. C. Currie, who has made a study of local history for years, is eminently qualified to do so. We hope one day to see a work of this kind published. We know it will do justice to the historic town which was established so long ago, in the heart of what was then a wilderness, beside the broad St. Lawrence.

AMONG THE THOUSAND ISLANDS

IX

Women Of Leeds

*And herein it is that I take upon me to make such a bold
assertion, That all the world are mistaken in their practice about
women. For I cannot think that GOD Almighty ever made them
so delicate, so glorious creatures; and furnished them with such
charms, so agreeable and so delightful to mankind; with souls
capable of the same accomplishments with men; and all, to be
only Stewards of our Houses, Cooks, and Slaves.*
                                        —DANIEL DEFOE.

THE ONLY WAY TO KNOW the real essence and
fabric of a country is to know the people. All too
often I have met those from other countries who had
not the least idea of what our people are really like. I
always wish I could have taken those visitors on a little

tour of Leeds, and that is why in print I am trying to make those from other regions understand our county. So now I am going to introduce to you some of the interesting women of Leeds.

Whenever I hear the term "farm woman," I am repelled. It does seem so utterly without allure. It just does not fit the modern countrywoman of Leeds; it sounds too drearily, repulsively dull. To me it calls up visions of a big, brawny, churn-like figure enveloped in a voluminous checked apron over a dour black dress, wearing shapeless old black boots, her stringy hair screwed up into a nubbin on the top of her head. Not but what I have known such women who, Heaven knows how, had retained a delightful philosophy and acquired a rich store of human knowledge, which made them the most comforting and heart-warming of persons to have around, especially in times of sickness and sorrow, which come to us all. But the average "farm woman" of today is something very different.

The very first women to come to Leeds were eventually farm women. They were extremely glad to become so. At first they were simply women camping in the bush. Many of them had been used to gentle living, comfortable surroundings and elegant clothes. A settler of this type, Mrs. Susanna Moodie, in her book, *Roughing It in the Bush,* describes the hardships met and endured even fifty or sixty years after the first English settlers took up land in the Province. They were indeed grateful when they had made a clearing in the bush, and could plant their crops and have a small farm. However, if they could come back today and visit the farms where their pioneer life began, they would in most cases find luxuries and conveniences which the well staffed country

FARM IN THE HINTERLANDS OF LEEDS

houses, in which many of them had been brought up, have never had, even to this present time.

The idea of the farm woman being a depressing specimen of humanity dies hard in the minds of the young people in some of our Canadian towns. A young country girl was entertaining some of her school friends in her attractive modern home, assisted by her mother, a smartly dressed, well educated little lady, who would have appeared to advantage in any house in the city.

"Why, I thought your mother would be a little old farm woman," later commented one of the guests. "You have a lovely home," she continued, still, apparently, somewhat surprised.

"We like it," was the only comment of the poised and unassuming young daughter of the house.

There are many such in the progressive county of Leeds. So, if you wish to travel about the county, here are some of the people you will meet.

My good friend, Marnie Davis, and I drove down the sixth concession four miles north of Lansdowne, along the Greenfield road. At our left the Blue Mountain formed a background for the comfortable homesteads of the district, as well as providing a supply of huckle- berries for the housewives' pies and preserves. Turning into a long lane, we arrived at a comfortable brick farm house with neat, well-kept grounds and big red barns. The lady of the house, Mrs. L. B. Webster, the former Julia Washburn, of Washburn's Corners, near Delta, came to the door. She is a pleasant, blue-eyed, brown- haired lady whose very appearance makes you feel that the kindest of hospitality is to be found within her home. She led us through a tidy summer kitchen, in one corner of which was a delightful century-old breakfront sideboard, handmade, into a red and white kitchen fitted with all modern conveniences, and so attractive that it might be envied by a woman of any city or town. Besides all the modern appurtenances which electricity brings, there was a well equipped bathroom and the pleasantest of dining and living rooms of ample size. The hot and cold running water was laid on upstairs and down. Both hard and soft water came out of the shining taps.

Putting some sandwiches in our pockets, we went in the farm truck as far as we could, and then walked the rest of the way over the lovely fields and through the thick woods of the Webster farm. Soon we came to the mountain ledges, where we saw strange and beautiful shrubs and plants not seen in the more cultivated lands. A porcupine sat so still on a branch just above our heads

that you would not know he breathed. The way grew
rougher and rougher; finally, after a rather rugged climb
we reached the top. It was autumn, and the glory of the
scene below can scarcely be described. For there, spread
out in a lovely pattern, were the blue, blue waters and
the multi-coloured islands of Charleston Lake. It is
almost like a view from an aeroplane at that height.
There was another group of people on the mountain
besides ourselves. It is a favourite climb on a Sunday,
especially in the fall.

When not caring for her home or "mountain climbing," Mrs. Webster has interests of many kinds. She
holds prominent offices in organizations such as the
Women's Institute and the Federation of Agriculture.
She has served on the School Area Board, and she is an
enthusiastic member of the Radio Farm Forum. Fond
of reading, she has an accurate grasp of current events
and is one of the most interesting speakers at local clubs.
She comes honestly by her aptitude in civic affairs; an
uncle, Luther Matthew Holton, was Minister of Finance
at one time.

Another woman who, like so many wives of farmers,
formerly taught school, lives on the pleasant Greenfield
road. She is Mrs. Carl Burns, who was Dorothy Andrew,
of Gananoque, a girl who had always lived in town. This
young woman loves her country home and would not
exchange it for one in town or city. No wonder she
prefers it, for it is one of the most attractive houses for
many miles. There are immense red barns; fir trees
involuntarily, "What a nice place to spend Christmas!
What a good time children would have in this place!"
cluster around the front windows of the house. You think

Mrs. Burns' little daughter is certainly fortunate in growing up in such a home.

Mrs. Burns is the great-great-granddaughter of Dr. W. Weeks, a U.E. Loyalist who, although born in England, was educated at Trinity University, Dublin. He first came to Vermont, but on arriving in Canada settled at MacIntosh's Mills, in Leeds County. Like many another descendant of the early pioneers, Mrs. Burns has achieved even more than the equivalent of comfort and luxury which her ancestors gave up for their loyalty to the Crown.

Mrs. Arthur Hudson, of Lyn, is a delightfully vivacious and interesting lady who adds colour to the local scene in Leeds. Born Evelyn Purvis, of Junetown, she is a great-granddaughter of Captain Peter Purvis, the doughty old elder of Brockville's First Presbyterian Church, who has come down in history as the gentleman who objected to what he called "feedlin' in the Hoose o' God." Striding down the aisle, he smashed the bow of the 'cello, which was being played by Mr. Richards in an attempt to liven things up.

Mrs. Hudson, still in the middle years, has crowded into those years a great deal of living. Married after a year of teaching, she brought up a sturdy family of three daughters and two sons, now all married but one. She is surrounded by a swarm of grandchildren, while still able to dash about hither and yon and enjoy every minute to the full. She, too, is always being elected to prominent positions in the same organizations as Mrs. Webster; she, too, has a beautifully decorated modern home. Lately, she and her husband have retired from active farming, but they did not move to town. They bought a nearby farmhouse and renovated it, while her husband began another interesting career. The eldest son remained on the home farm and carried on the work of operating it.

Mrs. Hudson also likes reading and is well up on current events. She is also much in demand as a speaker at various organizations, and on the Brockville programme, "Calling All Concessions." She practically commutes between Brockville and Toronto. Two married daughters live there, and she is always having to attend some important meeting of the Women's Institute or the Federation of Agriculture in that city. With all these activities, she finds time to do exquisite needlework, and have the daintiest of garments on hand for the latest grandchild. Definitely, she likes being a "farm woman" of Leeds.

Recently, she visited several countries of Europe as a W.I. delegate to the Convention of the Associated Countrywomen of the World.

It was afternoon of a day in late June. The Entrance class of little girls, ages ranging from eleven to fifteen, were having extra lessons after four. Among them was a little blonde, who was to be the wife of the present Principal of the Ottawa Normal School. The future Gananoque columnist was there, with long pigtails and a freckled nose. The young, blue-eyed teacher was also a dark blonde, slim and as neat as the proverbial pin. We sat on a little rise of ground in the grassy yard. Behind us was the old cemetery, among the crumbling stones of which we often played. Occasionally, we read the quaint verses dimly inscribed on the mossy stones. Lilacs and Balm of Gilead trees were haunted by plump golden orioles flitting about in the sunshine of that summer day, on the side of the picturesque hill named by an Irishman, William Webster, "Fair Dunciemaine," after a place in Ireland.

Our teacher, Mary Cochrane, now Mrs. Joseph Slack, had prepared us thoroughly for our Entrance examinations soon to be held in town. We loved the lessons in Literature, especially those held out of doors, most of all. Carefully we had learned all of Grey's "Elegy," and Stoke Poges was to us exactly like the little settlement near the old cemetery on the side of Dulcemaine Hill. As for the lines,

Ayr, gurgling, kissed his pebbled shore,
O'erhung with wild woods thick'ning green ...

to me they were the perfect description of scenes on Charleston Lake, and more especially of our own wild, lost shore. What wisdom our clever little teacher showed to have us hear these great lines of our poets in the warm, sweet air of those June afternoons!

Miss Cochrane was teaching at the age of sixteen, as she had trained when Gananoque had a Model School. Her first school was the white, blue-trimmed building at the Lyndhurst turn in Woodvale, where she met the man she married, Joseph Slack. This pioneer family then lived on the Charleston Lake shore, where the deserted farmhouse now stands. The family still own their original large tract of land. Mrs. Slack now lives on their farm near the Lansdowne turn. She has two stalwart sons, several grandchildren, and engages in many interesting activities.

A whole chapter could be written about the late Gertrude Bowen Webster, and also about a former resident, Lillian Collier Grey.

Gertrude Bowen Webster, wife of Wilfred, lived on the farm next to Mrs. L. B. Webster, in a charming, low, white frame house with a wide verandah. The mountain is a picturesque backdrop for Bluemont Farm, with its big red barns. She did all the work that a woman does on a farm, brought up a fine son, kept an immaculate house and entertained many friends. Besides all this, she wrote much splendid and melodious verse. She glorified the simple things of farm life which gave her comfort and pleasure as she went about her daily task. Lovely in mind and person, she has been greatly missed by all her wide circle of friends.

Lilian Collier Grey lived at Wilstead, in the old stone homestead in which W. J. Wilson (Billy) was born. I shall never forget the charm of her living room with its grey damask hangings, its fireplace and its many books. She, too, has written very fine verse, and, like Gertrude Bowen Webster, she writes of the simple things which are dear to the heart. She also helped to manage a large farm. Both successfully published books of poems. She now lives at Milton.

Nellie, as everyone calls little Mrs. George Daly, is a Dutch war bride who came to Lansdowne to marry the village druggist, whom she had met overseas. Her first husband, an officer, lost his life in the conflict, and she brought with her Toni, her "teen-ager" son. Mrs. Daly and Toni helped entertain the troops during the war, for they both are accomplished amateur actors and musicians. There is never a dull moment when this lively young woman is about the place. No wonder everyone calls her Nellie. She is just one of those people who have the gift of perpetual youth. Her gamin-like grin and exuberant spirits are infectious; she brightens up any party the minute she enters the room.

Excruciating are her chronicles of her struggles in learning to make a pie. She thought it must be easy.

"But no!" says Nellie. "I roll, I roll, I roll, I roll; my pie
go all to pieces. So I go over to see Mrs. Lochead. 'What's
the matter, Nellie?' she say, 'You look worried.' 'My
pie,' I say, 'it will not roll out.' So she take it and fix it,
and I watch, and I think, now I can make pie — but, no, it
is tough. George, he say it's all right, but I know better.
So I ask Mrs. Peck. 'You use too much water, Nellie,' she
say. Now I can make pie. Lots of pie. Is easy, now."

"Come over to my house for coffee," she said to
friends. "Thank you," they answered. "Are they coming?" asked her husband. "I do not think so," said Nellie.
"What did they say?" he enquired. "They say, 'Thank
you'," she replied. "Then they are coming," he told her.
Mrs. Daly would not believe it until she saw them. "What
did they thank me for?" she asked.

She knits the most intricately constructed sweaters
and makes the most fascinating hats. "I show you some
businesses," she said to me one evening, and in a minute
pranced in with one of the "businesses," a model of grey
felt flowers swathed in grey veiling, on her attractive
head. She makes them out of old felt hats.

As one might suspect, she has a French ancestor
away back, which accounts for her black hair, bright black
eyes and Gallic personality. She likes the village, and
they find her a decided asset to the community life.

Mrs. Charles (Denise) Lynch is a pretty Belgian war
bride, who lives in the same village. She, too, has many
useful accomplishments; she speaks several languages
and is an expert needlewoman. They were married in
Belgium during the last war. She likes our country but,
like Mrs. Daly, finds some of our ways and customs
strange. However, she loves living here and having her

own nice home. Slim, light-skinned and brown-haired, she wears her clothes extremely well and, like Mrs. Daly, would make a good model.

She is Flemish and comes from that part of Belgium. She speaks our language very well, and both she and Mrs. Daly have spoken in a most interesting and informative manner at various organizations. Her personality is also exuberant and vivacious. They do lend a new note of interest to the life of the village, these girls who are brides of the last war.

Mrs. Ernest Walmsley is the only woman in Leeds who lives in a house having radiant heating. There are only about a hundred so heated in Canada, I believe. Mr. Walmsley built his house where it commands a gorgeous view of the river, about two miles below Gananoque. They are both fond of country living, for themselves and for their children, and in the summer Mrs. Walmsley goes swimming twice a day.

In the winter they are always comfortable, no matter how great the cold. They prefer this system of heating to any other. In the summer, the house, with its picture windows and abundance of light and air, makes one feel as if he were living out in the fresh air with all the comforts found inside a house. It is extremely comfortable and attractive inside this unusual cinder block house, built all on the one level. There is a games room in the basement. It must be a very healthy place to live, and very easy to clean.

Mr. Walmsley is vice-president of the Parmenter and Bulloch Company of Gananoque, about which a great deal has been written in various periodicals, both American and Canadian, since it has been operated as a co-operatively owned concern. The president, who instigated this conversion, and under whom it is being so successfully managed, is T. J. Delaney.

I have often heard this lady of eighty-odd years speak of "Uncle Bill Gowan," for her aunt, Emily Taylor, married a man who was uncle to Emily Murphy, North America's first woman judge. Aunt Ell, as Mrs. Arthur McNichol, is usually called, is a granddaughter of Robert Taylor, who gave the land on which is situated the Union cemetery and the Union Church. Another native of Tilley, Senator George Taylor, saw that the cemetery was endowed, and consequently it is beautifully kept. His niece, Mrs. Janet Spence, of Brooklyn, gave hymn books and made many improvements in the interior of the church.

Aunt Ell lives alone in half of the old homestead at Escott, and is always ready to dispense hearty hospitality in her immaculate house. Many are the interesting relics of the past which she has treasured in this comfortable home throughout the years. Among them is a century-old Rose of Sharon quilt in perfect condition. Mrs. Hugh Reynolds, wife of the Conservative M.P.P., wants to take the pattern from it, she says with pride.

"I was born in that room upstairs, and there I mean to die," she says, with tranquil determination. Tall and distinguished looking, she is one of the few remaining members of a generation who accepted life with a placid serenity not often found in this modern world.

Leeds is noted for its many people who live to a great age. Not only do they live to be old, but many retain their faculties and enjoyment of life for an astonishing number

of years. Of such is a former teacher at the Brockville
Collegiate, Miss Edith Giles, now well on in her ninth
decade. She lives at Clone House, near the village of
Athens, on the Brockville road.

About a hundred and twenty years ago, Clone House
was built by William, grandfather of Edith Giles. He
called it after the estate in Ireland where he was born.
Clone means "garden in a meadow," and it is most suitably
named, for one can see pleasant meadows on every side,
and there are the most charming of Old World gardens
at the back of the low white house.

We entered the tree-shaded yard late one cloudy
evening, just before it began to rain. For a while we
lingered in the gardens, admiring the vegetables and
berry bushes, the old-fashioned flowers. Then, as it was
growing dark, we went inside.

Instantly we were transported into a Victorian
world. On the walls, old English prints and oil paintings
mingled with the family portraits collected through the
years. Some of the oil paintings were by the late
Crawford Slack. "He never took a lesson," said Miss
Giles, herself an art teacher and an art critic whose
opinion carries weight, "but his work is extremely good.
See those oil paintings over there?" she added. "They
were left here by a poor artist over a hundred years ago.
He never came back to claim them, and what became of
him I do not know."

The solid mahogany and walnut furniture had been
carefully selected, piece by piece. Much of it had come
from the British Isles. We admired the kidney shaped
sofa, the saddle back and Mary Pray chairs. One of the
most beautiful tables I have ever seen had a burl

mahogany top. A walnut glassed-in cabinet contained a large number of mugs brought from English towns. On each was the coat of arms belonging to the particular town from which it came. The collection belonged to Laura Cockill, the niece who now shares Miss Giles' home.

The beautifully carved dining room furniture is charming, as are the family portraits in antique frames which are on the walls. Dr. Giles' table desk remains as it was when in use for dispensing purposes, except for a coat of varnish which does not hide the scars. In the downstairs bedroom, furnished with walnut, were a dresser and two beds which had been made for Miss Giles' sister, Mrs. Cockill, out of the same log.

Mrs. Cockill, who married an Englishman, returned to Canada with her family after her husband's decease. Here she remained for the rest of her life, and many of the fine pieces of furniture brought over from England were hers.

Rare treasures were the fragile china cups and saucers without handles, the willow ware and lustre pitchers, the cruet stand with a design like silver lace. Cups did not have handles until the latter part of the eighteenth century, so those without are very old.

All the time we had been seeing the house and its treasures, the rain had been pouring down. It was falling in thick grey sheets when we left. To our amazement, we found that hours had passed and it was eleven o'clock. So, if you wish to while away a rainy summer evening, do go and see lovely old Clone House, the home of Miss Edith Giles.

"Aunt Nell," as they call Mrs. C. F. Moulton, is one of the most interesting ladies in Leeds. She is the capable and beloved proprietress of Charleston's Harbour View Hotel, a description of which is found in another chapter. The guests are like a big family presided over by the motherly "Aunt Nell." Born Nell Hudson, in a pretty frame farmhouse two miles away, she got her training in the hotel business with Mr. L. Southworth, when he ran the old Cedar Park Hotel.

"My, he was the grand man," she recalls. "It was a sight to see him sweep across the lobby among his guests in his Prince Albert coat."

Aunt Nell's recipes are carefully followed in her cuisine; her pies melt in your mouth. It is a fine place to have dinner after a drive through the wilder parts of the hinterlands of Leeds. Not only will you have a delicious meal, but you will have the privilege of meeting that interesting personality, "Aunt Nell."

There was an era in which many daughters of large landowners in the county were brought up in such a manner that they became gentlewomen in the truest and most unpretentious sense of the word. For many a long year the memory and influence of such a person, the late Anna Kate Shaw, nee Mallory, widow of Dr. John M. Shaw, will remain. This tall, white-haired lady was one of those who helped give a distinctive background to Leeds. Afternoons she sat placidly in the long room which, with its solid walnut furniture, milk glass lamps, heavy gilt frames and other effects belonging to a late Victorian era, was more like an old-time drawing room than the more informal living room of today, and friends came in to talk quietly, enjoying her placidity and dry, shrewd wit. All her eighty-seven years she savoured life with quiet relish and took part in many activities almost to the last.

She was more a Georgian than a Victorian; for there was about her no affectation and nothing of the hypocritical prude. A spade was a spade, but a casually well-bred spade, and no fuss about it at that. She and Mrs. Darling founded the Lansdowne Literary Society, which has been functioning for over thirty years. It is, as far as I know, the only one of its kind in Leeds. She was the last of a type which we no longer know.

In a small village of Leeds lives Mrs. A. Mallory, nee Cassie Purvis, a great-aunt of Barbara Ann Scott. Mrs. Mallory was young in the last of the Victorian era; she is of Scottish extraction, although very far back it was really French. Maybe one reason Barbara Ann is so dainty and petite is that ancient, but persistent, French strain. She was born on a Canadian farm. Her house reflects her unassuming and extremely witty personality. It is set in cool, terraced lawns surrounded by a low stone wall; the rooms are full of charm. It is a perfect example of the better type of late Victorian house, without the smothered effect which they sometimes acquired. The polished grand piano, saddleback chairs and other solid walnut pieces of furniture, the cut glass and old silver, the wide bay windows, all create an atmosphere of restful ease. Upstairs is a trunkful of the precious handwoven quilts in blue and white design. In perfect condition, they are over a hundred years old. Mrs. Mallory, who belongs to the generation when well brought up young ladies attended all dances in long white kid gloves, has a personality which combines the charm of the sheltered lady with the witty worldliness and the practical viewpoint of the modern world. In her youth, she must have borne a strong resemblance to Barbara Ann. Their profiles are startlingly alike.

One of those who recently came to live in our county is Mrs. Richard Duff, wife of the editor of The Lansdowne *Reporter*. She was formerly Mary Brown, and was born at Brandon, Manitoba, but the family moved to Hespeler, Ontario, when she was a year old. There she was educated and became an examiner of textiles in the Dominion Woollen Company, the third largest in Canada. She was organist in St. James' Anglican Church for several years, inheriting her musical talent, no doubt, from her grandfather Brown, who was an organist in Malvern, England, for a period of sixty years. Treasured by Mrs. Duff is the programme used for his memorial service, when they unveiled a plaque to his memory.

Mr. Duff met her in October; they were married in June. A quiet, restful person with dark eyes and a sweet, shy expression, just plump enough to be the cosy type, she makes a delicious cup of tea. Fond of knitting, she knits her husband gorgeous diamond socks. She and Mr. Duff, like so many newcomers, have seen more of the lovely country around here than people who have lived here for years. We are so used to it that we do not always appreciate it. They see it with new eyes. Mrs. Duff is the kind of person whose coming enriches the life of any community, especially a small village. "I love Lansdowne," she says. "The people are so kind." Lansdowne folks are, we know, glad that it is with them that such a desirable newcomer has made her home.

Roxey McCrady is a happy spinster of unique personality. Few glamour gals have been so loved and admired. She was a frail little body, who carried a heavy burden of responsibility upon her all through her youth, and even into late middle age. She would come to us and other families and stay a week, making all kinds of garments for everyone in the family, and surrounded by an adoring circle of children who must have been the most frightful nuisance, but of whose company she never seemed to tire. She didn't talk down to us, but she always seemed to be exactly our own age. Next to Mother, there was no one who appeared to consider us so important or who understood us so well. Although she was thin, she was a restful soul, with a placid disposition, and she made life look so interesting, I don't quite know how. At parties she was immensely popular, for she had Cinderella feet and could move as lightly as a piece of thistledown through a lively square. The young men of the neighborhood thought her lots of fun, she was so lively and ready for a good joke. Her life was not easy, but no one ever heard her complain. Sundays she was a regular attendant at her church. Late in life she became a most efficient practical nurse, assisting into the world several hundred babies of Leeds. She's still lively, she's still nursing, and between times sewing and helping others in various ways. I have known quite a few wealthy people, but I have never known one who got as much out of life as she. Even now, well on in her eighth decade, she is still one of the busiest and happiest women of Leeds.

Toward the close of the nineteenth century, a tall, slender, attractive young girl, golden-haired and hazel-eyed, hung up her shingle on King Street in Gananoque, about where the James Cafe now stands. She was educated in the Athens High and Model Schools, and for several years taught school. By practising the strictest economy, she managed to put herself through Queen's University, finishing her course at the University of Toronto. This was not too easy an accomplishment in those times, when the few women who went in for

medicine did not find the men taking the course too
kindly disposed toward the idea. But Dr. Annie Mc-
Callum's Highland Scotch ancestry stood her in good
stead. She persevered, and graduated to become an
outstanding success in her profession.

She married Dr. Alden Alguire, a member of a
pioneer family long known in Leeds. After practising
medicine for a time in Gananoque, they left to settle
permanently in Belvidere, Illinois. There both achieved
marked success, Dr. Alden being interested in art and
literature and doing creditable work in that line himself,
Dr. Annie composing the words and music for songs
during both wars. One song composed during World War
II was sung on the radio by a noted artist. She also
invented clever and useful gadgets. She and Dr. Alden
built a hospital, which stands as a monument to their
years of service.

Over a decade ago she visited the continent and the
British Isles, especially enjoying her stay in Scotland, the
country of her mother's birth. "There's going to be a
war. The older people in Germany are all so sad," she
said when she came back. It was not long until the war
began. When she returned, she had to repeat her
lecture on her trip before all the folk of Belvidere who
wished were able to hear it. Dr. Alden is no longer
living. Dr. Annie, indomitable and interested in this
modern world at over eighty, practised her profession
until shortly before she died. Until late in the thirties,
she drove to Canada every few years. Among the many
guests who come and go during one's childhood on an old
Ontario farm, there are some who have such glamour
that their coming is an event. The golden-haired Dr.
Annie, my mother's lifelong friend, was one of these.

Miss Rebecca Edwards has in Blinkbonnie created an atmosphere of a fascinating Canadian era. It was this former teacher of art who encouraged E. Grace Coombs to persevere in her work when she was a student in the Gananoque High School, and to her and the Misses Stunden, who kept a very excellent private school, belongs part of the credit for her success. Visitors to Blinkbonnie must come away convinced that we really have a Canadian culture. In some of the rooms are lovely pieces of furniture which belonged to the family of Joel Stone.

Gracious, white-heared Mrs. Catherine Runyon spreads an atmosphere of serenity around the famed Golden Apple, whose buildings are furnished with fine antiques in the most exquisite taste. An American, the daughter of Governor Flower, she has been operating the hostelry for over twenty years. So fond is she of the town that she now spends the winters here as well. She is beloved by all about the place.

Another whose personality enlivens the scene is Mrs. Florence Harris, who, with her husband, Albert, helps run the ménage. This cheery-faced lady and her adjutant, Mrs. Nellie Munden, whom everyone affectionately calls "Nell" (she's a Devonshire lass) would make anyone feel at home. But Mr. Toots, our cocker spaniel, is absolutely devoted to Mrs. Munden's sister, Mrs. Dorothy Smith; she's his favourite lady; but they are all so good to him, the kind chefs, the chauffeur and everyone, with their gifts of nice, juicy bones.

This is supposed to be a chapter about women, but Mr. A. Harris and Noah Gauthier are used to being surrounded by women, so I'll put them in. They'll be right at home.

Tall, silver-haired Mr. Harris can turn in with a chef's cap on his head and give a hand, or go out in a Homburg and black overcoat, looking like the owner of an Old Country estate. Incidentally, Bobbie Burns wrote a poem about Mrs. Harris' grandfather, Robert Graham, Esq.

Noah Gauthier is the major-domo of the place. You just couldn't imagine it without him. Over seventy, with his satellites, Sandy McDonald and Harry Bovey, he buzzes about like mad from April to October, when the Golden Apple is closed for the season. He seems to know all about everything and to be everywhere at once. It is impossible to think of anyone taking his place.

André tells the most accurate fortunes ever known, which provide much excitement for the guests of the Golden Apple.

There once was "Sandy," the overstuffed golden retriever, a dog with an air of dignity in keeping with the place; but he is no more, and is much missed.

Genevieve Ledger, the hostess, recently married to John Joseph Jordan, is a true Celtic type. Black hair and dark eyes, it was from Ireland many of her people came. For she is, on her mother's side, of the O'Sullivan clan who settled in a log homestead in a valley near Charleston Lake, which must have reminded them of Killarney, from which region they probably came. The family of girls were true Irish beauties, white-skinned and dark-eyed, and they used to walk every Sunday the four long miles to Mass. The smartly dressed Miss Ledger, a most attractive and gracious hostess, helps give a feeling of hospitality to the place.

That remarkably energetic lady, Miss Grace Landon, runs a guest house, The Landon, with an Old World background, all unaided except for the assistance of her mother, a rosy-cheeked lady far along in her eighties. The building is very old and very large, but well preserved. Of beige stucco trimmed with green, it has one of the largest and most attractive verandahs in town. The immaculate interior is beautifully furnished in period pieces in keeping with the house.

For several years the vivacious mistress of Currie Manor welcomed guests with true Irish hospitality, for it was in Ireland that she was born. Her husband bears a startling resemblance to his cousin, the late Sir Sam Hughes, of the first World War fame. Currie Manor also has a broad, shady verandah where the guests love to take their ease. Recently the Careys, who also make people feel very much at home, have purchased the place. Mr. Carey was formerly in the Department of Travel and Publicity.

I first saw Dr. Sue Thompson Gould when, in the little village of Delta, we attended a meeting of the Teachers' Institute. She was a peppy, brown-haired girl whom you knew would reach whatever goal she had in mind. Definitely, she did.

She was born on an old homestead near Gananoque, in the vicinity of South Lake. After teaching for some time, she decided to become a doctor, and is a graduate of the University of Chicago and Rush Medical College, Chicago, and of the University of Michigan, Ann Arbor. For some years she was school physician at Gary, Indiana, and associate director of the Bureau of Maternal and Child Health, Michigan Department of Health, as well as Director of District Health Unit of West Branch, Michigan. In 1945 she married Edward Henry Gould, of New York City. She and her husband take a deep interest in literature and the arts, and all things pertaining to adult education. She has had an extremely interesting and successful career, has little Susie Thompson, of Leeds.

Mrs. Sandford Delaney, born Eva Bradley, of Escott, has lived in Gananaque for many years. In fact, she has the distinction of being one of Gananoque's first career women; she was a member of the Town Council for several terms. After she became a widow, during the second World War, she managed the Delaney Theatre herself, for her stalwart sons were overseas. Married very young, she is the mother of twelve children, nine of whom are living. With the help of one maid, she cares for the large, attractive home near the river, and takes in tourists as well.

Sundays finds her faithfully performing her duties as organist in St. John's Roman Catholic Church. She has a lovely voice, so she is much in demand as a soloist at weddings and other festivities. Part of the time she has an agency for women's accessories. I do not know what she does in her spare time.

All but one of her six sons live in Gananoque; all but one of her sons and one daughter are married. She has been a grandmother many times. Still youthful looking and fond of gaiety, this vivacious lady loves to drive her car expertly; she can also dance like mad. Life will always be full of interest to this spirited woman of Leeds.

There are many other women of Leeds of whom I should like to write. There is that former resident, Mrs. Arthur (Minnie) Purvis, mother of the late Dr. Leonard Purvis. Widowed early in life, this gallant lady brought up her family of four sons, thinking nothing of tackling the most arduous tasks. She learned to drive a car when over sixty; she drove for nearly twenty years. House after house in which she lived she painted and papered, making them into attractive homes. She loved to take friends out in her car. When about seventy-five she drove from Lyn to Ottawa over icy roads to spend Christmas with her son. Now her sons are gone and, in her eighties, she lives with her memories of the years. Friends and relatives recall with pleasure her sojourn in Leeds.

I would like to write of the late Dr. Elizabeth Beatty and of Irene Stringer, Presbyterian missionaries who went out to India from Lansdowne; of the late Louise McKinney of the Crummy family. The latter was born in a homey brick house near Athens and was the first woman in the British Empire to be a member of the Legislative Assembly. Another interesting personality is Mrs. George T. Fulford, who does many kindly deeds so unobtrusively. Also in Brockville is a career woman, Janice Delahaye, whose smart shop cannot be equalled in many towns and cities. Then there is Mrs. Harris McNish, who was a war bride of the first Great War, and who lives in one of the prettiest homes in Leeds. Up in the rugged hills of Sand Bay is Mrs. Wilfrid Fodey, who has taught school so long and happily, besides running a farm. Down along the river is that cosy lady, Mrs. Gerald Shipman, to whose well-known summer resort I once hurried at midnight to see a giant night-blooming cereus slowly unfold no less than seventeen exotic blossoms. The heady perfume was enchanting on the river breeze. Of these and many others I should like to write, if ever I do another book about Leeds.

X

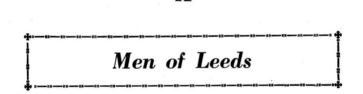

Men of Leeds

Character is nature in its highest form. It is of no use to ape it or to contend with it. Somewhat is possible of resistance, and of persistence, and of creation, to this power, which will foil all emulation.

RALPH WALDO EMERSON.

T J. STOREY WAS A MAN who lived one of the fullest and most complete lives I have ever known. • Born one of several children in a none too affluent Irish-Canadian family, he was determined from the time he was a small boy to make good. And to his credit, not to make good only in a material way, but to get out of life all that adds to the fullness and richness of living. In all his ninety years, he probably never knew a moment's boredom.

It would take a book to do full justice to his life. This is only a brief sketch of the qualities of the man, and some of the highlights of his career. He was born in the little hamlet of Escott, and learned general repair work in his father's shop. When his family moved to Gananoque, he worked after school and on Saturdays in various industrial concerns. After a while he was employed in the Brockville Carriage Works; finally he and his friends decided to open a shop in Gananoque, where they did all sorts of repair and decorative work, eventually opening several shops in different villages.

One day, when he and his brother were walking down street, they met two young girls. One was very pretty, indeed beautiful, with her slender figure, fine features and long black ringlets swinging as she walked. She wore a freshly starched pink chambray dress.

"There," said T. J., after they passed, "is the girl I'm going to marry."

"Funny she didn't speak to you," observed his brother, surprised.

"Oh, I don't know her yet," said T. J., with the utmost unconcern.

They were married several years later, after he had repaired for occupation a house that was to have been pulled down. It was to last for fifty years.

Finally Mr. Storey returned to the Brockville Carriage Works. Eventually he became its head. Later he moved to Montreal, where he spent many years in important concerns. He crossed the ocean more than twenty times. He had an audience with King George the Fifth, and with his family attended a garden party at Buckingham Palace. Owners of great estates enjoyed his

DINNY IS TIMELESS

visits, his pithy sayings, his homely wit. He began to collect antiques and to take an interest in art. All his life he was a great reader, buying what books he could in his early days, procuring others from friends or from the Public Library.

Although very successful, success never went to his head, and he was loved by those who worked under him. He was always simple, unaffected and kind. Sorrow came to him in the loss of a beautiful daughter in her 'teens. A son is a prominent business man in the West, and another daughter is the wife of Canada's trade commissioner to Mexico, Douglas Cole.

When he was eighty. he retired to the picture-book village of Lyn. There he and his wife lived quietly and happily until she passed away, leaving him alone with his memories. However, he found some comfort in his beautiful terraced garden, in making fine pieces of furniture out of old pianos, and in painting very creditable

landscapes in oils. Occasionally he dined out with some
of his friends. Every year he opened "Rocklyn," his
spacious home, to the people for his birthday celebration.
The last, his ninetieth, was the best of all. T. J., moving
happily about in cream flannel trousers and white shirt,
didn't look a day over sixty-five. There were oceans of
good things to eat; in a tent was a band. Crowds of
people swarmed about the lawn. There were telegrams
from many notables, including (and this was the subject
of good-natured kidding, T. J. being a Conservative of the
dyed-in-the-wool kind) one from Prime Minister Mackenzie King. T. J. replied to all the tributes he received
with some emotion. His usually firm voice faltered at
the last; there were tears in his eyes.

For many years T. J. had driven back and forth to
Florida, even in his ninetieth spring. Now in September
he was planning to go to Montreal to get a new car. One
soft September afternoon, when the breeze sighed gently
over the willow-swept pond, the housekeeper went in to
see if he had awakened from his afternoon nap. But T. J.
had not awakened. There he lay, his passing as peaceful
as his kindly life.

He's a country doctor, but put him on Fifth Avenue
and the only difference you would notice would be that
he was better tailored than the majority of men on the
street. He has the kind of sturdy appearance and strong
jaw you usually associate with a man of Scottish descent.
He is not too great a talker, but his smile lights up his
face, giving it a hearty warmth and kindliness, which
often does his patients as much good as dozens of big
brown pills. Days, and often nights, he is hard at work.
When other folk are home in their snug warm beds, he

is out in the wilder parts of the county, in places where, in order to get through, he may have to shovel part of the roads. He must be ready for any emergency. I have known him to bring a child into the world in a hut where there were only newspapers, no sheets or towels. Seldom does he lose a case. One reason for this is that he does not allow himself to lag behind in his professional knowledge. He learns all he can about new drugs and techniques. He is not conceited or superior, he has no heavy professional manner such as was in vogue in Victorian times, and the poorest and most unfortunate know he is their friend. There are many like him in Canada, but the individual I have described is one of the best.

The great Cardinal Wolsey lived like a prince in his palace at Hampton Court. It was huge, a thousand spacious, high-ceilinged rooms. On its walls are some of the most beautiful paintings I have ever seen. There are lovely formal gardens, an indoor tennis court, and the famous maze which is so confusing. It was not, in Wolsey's day, exactly a monastic ménage. At that time, the early part of the sixteenth century, the great prelates of the Church were not expected to live an entirely celibate life. One of the ladies admired by the Cardinal was married off to a yeoman of good family. A yeoman was then, even as now, a farmer who owned his own land instead of having a ninety-nine year lease, as do the majority of British farmers. If his place were large, he was often considered as ranking next to the titled classes. So it was a good match. The descendant of this beauty became a famous Southern general in the war between the North and the South. The general's first cousin, twice removed, lives in a two-roomed cottage on a hill in one of the more rugged parts of Leeds.

He's a sturdy, fine-looking gentleman for all of his seventy-five years, this descendant of a lady who found favour in the great Cardinal's eyes. His dark eyes are still bright with his deep interest in all that goes to make up life. The little house is snug and cosy. The Axminster carpet stretches to the very door. There is a bookcase filled with books, including a large family Bible and a Concordance; for this interesting man is a great student of Holy Writ.

Mr. Asher Lee is also an amateur geologist. Living near one of the most beautiful lakes in Canada, probably of glacial origin, he is able to find many intriguing specimens right in his own back yard. He has a splendid collection of petrified wood, one piece showing a screw imbedded in it. There are arrow heads and pieces of flint, the substitute for matches in primitive times. An old coffee grinder in his possession has been in the family for two hundred years.

Most older men do not care for new schemes, but are cautions and attached to the old ways. He is always thinking up some new device, such as a combine to work for the whole district or a community deep freezing locker.

He has so many hobbies and interests, he is never bored; and that, one thinks, must be the secret of a happy old age.

William Vanderburg and Samuel Horton will always be remembered as the men who first thought of developing the Outlet, but the cottages of Fred McConnell, of

Lansdowne, and his family, have greatly beautified the shore opposite Greer's Point. All the McConnells (there are just ten of them) have been coming there for years. In almost any season they may be found prowling happily about this, their favourite corner of all the earth.

An enterprising group of Americans, assisted by Percy Earle, of Lansdowne, and James Purvis, of Kemptville, have opened up the absolutely fascinating "Burma Road;" the entrance is near Dinny's shack.

Ireland was the home of Alex Steacy's ancestors, and before that, England, so he is one of the numerous Anglo-Irish who farm in Leeds. He is a good example of a stalwart modern agriculturist of Leeds. He went to High School, uses good English, and he and his wife, the former Marian Webster, are ardent supporters of the Radio Farm Forum, Adult Education courses, Federation of Agriculture and all projects for the public good. Most city dwellers would envy them their home, which has all the conveniences which help to lessen the work of the farm. Many of the owners of small estates in the Old Country have not as pleasant surroundings or as many conveniences as these. The house is a good distance from the barns, which are also well built. The fields are broad and level, and there are pleasant woods. All around are other well cultivated and attractive homesteads.

This man is of a type found rather often in Leeds. He works hard, but he has security and great comfort, as well as plenty of recreation, for towns are quickly reached by car. His is a satisfying way of life. I doubt he has ever regretted that he decided to farm.

For forty-five years an extremely successful Canadian industrialist has been coming to his summer home on one of the loveliest islands in the heart of the Thousand Islands. The house is pine panelled, mellowed by time, and has a picturesque background of rocky hills and trees. There is a magnificent spruce, which has reached a great height in its half century of growth. No attempt at formal landscaping has, fortunately, been made, but little crooked paths wander here and there among the beds of brilliant flowers. Quaint stone steps ascend the little hills. The owner can, with humorous mock impressiveness, recite all the long botanical names of every flower and shrub.

When you take the tour of the Thousand Islands, this house of many rooms is pointed out as a show place. What they do not know is that it is also a home place. Generations of comfortable, happy living have flavoured the very air.

Interesting small cottages for various members of the family are partially concealed among the shrubbery. One is equipped for amateur photography and for minor repairs for household appliances. It has a corner cupboard in which are pretty coloured dishes and other necessities for afternoon tea. There is also a tea house in which one member of the family loved to have her friends for tea in days gone by. It is so arranged that they could have their tea in the open while they enjoyed the view of the quiet water and the islands beyond.

A dwelling which is a real home place must have three things in harmony — the landscape, the house and the people. Here this happy effect is achieved. The house, with its muted green and rust shades, blends into the wild Canadian landscape. Around it are wide, hospitable verandahs.

The large, cool rooms are comfortably, but not ostentatiously, furnished. Restful divans, chairs and couches are placed where they are most convenient. Here and there, in nearly every room, are fascinating combinations of shelves of books, with pieces of attractive china. The pictures are of a period in keeping with the house, some collected by the owner during his Oxford days.

Many windows give a feeling of freedom as well as plenty of light and air. One group of windows looks down into sombre green waters.

They stay here until late in the fall. When it is too cold to play tennis or swim, they can be very comfortable in the living room, listening to the radio, playing the piano, or just reading one of their many good books.

I have never enjoyed afternoon tea more than in these interesting surroundings, where I met a young lady from Ireland with a delightful accent, and a cousin of author Sheila Kaye-Smith, who owns some pieces of furniture which once belonged to Charlotte Bronte, author of *Jane Eyre*

This household, with its rather patriarchal life, is like an island Jalna in many ways. The head bears so very lightly his unsuspected years, and loves to gather about him the members of his clan.

They are all fond of exploring Leeds, and the amateur photographer has some very fine pictures of its lovely wilds.

It was a bitterly cold winter night, and the brightly lighted windows of the little school at the crossroads looked very inviting to those who were coming in out of the cold. For many weeks an earnest revival had been going on, and many souls had been brought to feel the need of a more personal faith in God. As was usual in those times, a fun-loving group of boys came to stand outside, peer in through the windows, and try by their antics to make the less serious-minded laugh. Among them was a sturdy young fellow, so well developed that he looked several years older than his seventeen years, who was the biggest daredevil of them all. One night he was outside pulling the most ludicrous faces to make the young folk laugh, the next night, he never quite knew why, he went inside. Now, if anyone in that congregation had been asked who was the person least likely to become the most noted evangelist of that area, he would have answered that it was this handsome, reckless fellow. He was not wicked, but he craved excitement. Not for him the staid ways of the established faiths. He was eager to taste all the sensations of life, to know how it felt to take a little too much to drink, to smoke a strong-smelling pipe, and to perform all sorts of high-spirited pranks. However, not even Paul, who on the way to Damascus was blinded by a great light, had a greater revelation than he. Suddenly he had an uncontrollable desire to go forward to the "mercy seat," and with streaming eyes, confess his sins. But a great chunk of wood beside the old box stove was in his path. Could he, in his emotional condition, pass it without falling over it? For a moment he thought he could not. Then, to the utter amazement of his lively companions, he arose and with firm, manly tread went forward and sank upon his knees. At first many were skeptical of his conversion, but as days went on it became apparent, even to the most doubting, that he had begun a new life. He threw away his pipe, he did not drink, and he made restitution for some of his youthful pranks. In a year or so he married one of the loveliest girls in Leeds. Soon he became a preacher and an evangelist of ability and power, for he had the magnetic personality which draws a crowd. Eventually he was ordained. All his life he will marvel at the strangeness of the ways of God.

Leeds County has not many millionaires, but there is one who has a British Empire look, who is known everywhere and liked wherever he goes. Many millions and unusual opportunities have not changed the character of this stalwart, easy-going gentleman in his forties. The men usually call him by his first name. Nor does this denote familiarity; in spite of his unassuming manners, he commands as much respect as if the name were preceded by the "Sir" of an Old Country village squire. He is of the old pioneer stock, which is probably one of the reasons great wealth has never turned his head. He has cousins who operate some of the finest farms in this county. His helpmeet has the same unassuming, kindly manners, and helpful concern for those to whom fortune has not been kind.

Mixing sociably with the people, this broad-shouldered, grey-coated figure may be seen at country socials or fall fairs, and he always seems to be having a grand time. He is just as much at home talking to the most old-fashioned farmer as when entertaining a governor-general or an English prince. He is at present at the height of a successful political career. Communism would receive a set-back if there were more men of his type. We are glad he belongs to Leeds.

Canada's "Who's Who" does not list too many men who are noted for anything except success in business. Among the few who are so honoured for their achievements in the arts and letters is Lorne Pierce, a well known native of Leeds County, who for over thirty years has been editor of The Ryerson Press, the oldest and largest publishing house of Canada.

He was born in the village of Delta, in the last decade of Victoria's reign. His parents, Edward and Harriet Louise (Singleton) Pierce, were both of Anglo-Irish descent. Dr. Pierce's great-grandmother, Sara Anne Butler, was one of the romantic young girls who eloped from Ireland and settled in the county of Leeds. Her husband, young Thomas Singleton, of County Wexford, fought in the continental Wars, and afterward was a tutor in the family of the Butlers of Dublin, one of the most ancient titled families of Ireland. From his maternal grandmother he picked up some English and Scots blood, which perhaps accounts for the sound business sense which, combined with a romantic sensitivity to the imaginative and the fine in art and life, helped to make his career a success.

Lorne Pierce spent his youth in the lovely old village of Delta and attended Athens High School. His mother must have been what the old-fashioned novelists called "a woman of parts." She it was who taught him and his sister, Sara, to love all that was best in literature and the arts. She had a fine library, was a talented musician and painted on glass and canvas for many years. The family read the standard novelists and poets at an early age, each taking turns in reading aloud. Dr. Pierce says, "I did not like reading when I was very young." "How old were you when you began to like to read?" I enquired, thinking he would be about seventeen. "Nine," he replied, solemnly and regretfully. At the age of ten he began to buy books, his first purchase being **Paradise Lost,** and the next a volume of Keats. That this gifted writer and publisher is the kind of man he is must be in a measure due to the background created by that unusual woman, Harriet Louise Pierce.

After graduating from Queen's, where his sister also attended, he went on to Victoria College, Toronto, Union Theological Seminary, New York, New York University, and the United Theological College, affiliated with McGill University. In 1916 he was ordained to the ministry of the Methodist Church, and in the same year married a bright and charming young lady, Edith Chown, of Kingston, whom he had met at Queen's. His first pastorate was St. James, Ottawa, which he resigned to enlist as a private in World War I, but was unable to get to the front. In his next pastorate, in Matilda Township, Dundas County, he founded one of the first and most successful Rural Community Centres in Canada, which became the official rural programme of the Methodist Church of Canada, and was widely copied. It was while serving at Brinston that he was offered the editorship of the Methodist Book and Publishing House.

It was a wonderful time to be an editor of such a House as Ryerson's, the trade name given to the firm in 1920, almost 100 years after its founding. For one thing the famous Group of Seven was causing a revolution in Canadian Art, while the founding of the Canadian Authors' Association foretold impressive developments in Canadian letters. The whole country was tingling with new life, a native culture was at last taking shape, and it was a thrilling thing to be a part of it. Most of those who were leaders in this great creative period were personal friends of Lorne Pierce.

Chapters could be written about the life of this interesting Canadian and his gracious wife, who has a wonderful time following up her hobby of collecting old glass, experimenting with her potter's wheel, mothering her Red Cross girls at Sunnybrook Hospital, and sharing the career of her husband. Dr. Pierce has founded the Gold Medal of the Royal Society of Canada which bears his name, awarded to Canadians whose total achievement in letters is of outstanding importance. He has also given to Queen's University a collection of Canadiana of great value to students, and has endowed it with a trust most fittingly named after his wife. Dr. Pierce has written many books and edited many more, the list being too long to name here. He has served the arts and letters of Canada, east and west, French and English, and has received many honours from universities and societies. He regards as perhaps a kindly dispensation of Providence that his defective hearing (he wears a hearing aid) made it impossible to follow his first beloved vocation, the ministry. A new life and ministry was opened up for him in which his disability was not a handicap. In fact, as one of the founders of The National Society of the Deaf and the Hard of Hearing his own handicap opened a great field of national service.

Dr. and Mrs. Pierce have two children, Beth and Bruce, both graduates of the University of Toronto, both married to graduates of the same university. Their grandchildren are the sixth generation to walk beside the lovely Beverley Lakes, where the family have a summer home, "Windrush."

Rain or shine, Mr. Frank Wright may be seen every morning taking a stroll down the main street of Gananoque. He is eighty-five, but many a man half his age has not as much zest for life. For Mr. Wright has so many interests that time has never hung heavy on his hands. Always he has found the universe full of wonder and variety.

He is the son of Robert Wright and Elizabeth Slack, of Yorkshire extraction on his father's side and Dutch Puritan U.E. Loyalist stock on the maternal side. The house now occupied by Mr. Mills on the east corner of Garden Street was surrounded by an orchard when he was born there in 1867.

When he was big enough to wield a paint brush, he left school. He made his living by that occupation until ten years ago. He was incapacitated by an accident, or he would probably be painting yet. He also did a great deal of papering in the houses of the town.

But what Mr. Wright is chiefly noted for is his knowledge of local history. He is a regular encyclopaedia when it comes to the events of the past. He has a small museum of interesting objects, such as ancient tiles, old Roman coins and firearms.

He did want to go to Lansdowne Fair about four years ago, when he was only eighty-one. There was a booth which had some antiques in it which he wished to see. So he hitch-hiked the ten long miles.

Except that he has to wear a hearing aid, he is in rather good health. Last summer he and Mrs. Wright, a pretty lady with dark eyes and white hair, celebrated their diamond wedding. He was married at twenty-two. One son, Claude Millard, lost his life in World War I, another, Captain Franklin Ellis, in World War II.

There are valleys where the memory lingers, and where much good, deep living has given a flavour to the surroundings which, though very real, it is difficult to describe.

Nearly every evening, in this particular valley, a car drives quietly up the red gravel road, past the fir-edged lawn and the rows of brightly nodding flowers, and an older man in grey, carrying a brief case, climbs slowly out and enters his cheerful domain. A sense of mellow timelessness and security pervades the comfortable rooms.

This bachelor, who has not farmed for many years, would not exchange his country home for the grandest mansion in town, and thinks it well worth returning to, although it means a drive of over fifteen miles. Here is his own land, many acres of it; here have flourished his roots for more than a hundred and twenty-five years. Inside are quiet-voiced members of his family, the well cooked food which cannot be found in restaurants, good music and many books. There are frequent visitors who always return. Little dinner parties find them lingering at the table for hours, enjoying stimulating conversation on topics which have a wide range. They adore Dickens and Scott; indeed, a not too remote ancestor was a niece of a prominent character in a well known novel. Their knowledge of Shakespeare would put many college graduates to scorn. They are the kind of farming people of whom visitors never hear — the kind who came from the county families or the professional class of the Old Land to be pioneers in the New. A certain tradition of culture prevailed, even though there were not many facilities for a formal education for more than a hundred years. All over Canada these farm homes exist. They can certainly be found in Leeds.

This gentleman of Scotch-Irish extraction always thinks of himself as a farmer. He would be surprised and probably offended to be told that he has been an unofficial country gentleman for many years.

It was a warm day, and as we passed the small shack near the rushes of the bay we noticed a pair of feet clad in socks protruding beyond the open door. Dinny was having a nap, and part of his length was outside his house, as was necessary if he lay on the floor. Outside also was the cook stove, so that the shack would be cooler in the hot summer days.

In the tourist season, Dinny may still be seen rowing fishermen up and down Charleston Lake. Usually he wears a red plaid shirt; occasionally he sports one that is surprisingly white. His age is uncertain, but he must be nearly ninety. Of his racial origin, however, there can be no doubt. The cadences of old Ireland are in his soft, ingratiating voice.

He, for one, has solved the problem of the high cost of living. In the spring, he opens the door of his shack near the rushes and waits for the fish to swim in. Then he shuts the door and has fish for dinner. When the floor is dry he sprinkles crumbs on it, and again leaves the door carelessly ajar. Result — chicken dinner for Dinny. Driftwood provides his fuel.

Epic are some of the tales which he tells, or which are told about him by some of his friends. There was, for instance, the affair of the thieving rooster.

"I looks out the window," said Dinny, "and sees him slingin' the inyins (onions) over his shoulder. So I says to Mrs. B. 'Your rooster is stealin' my inyins.' 'Oh, but

I have no rooster!' says Mrs. B. Next day I looks out again, and there he is, slingin' the inyins over his shoulder faster than ever. So I gets my little twenty-two, and I shoots the rooster. Out comes Mrs. B. 'You shot my rooster!' she hollers. 'You'll pay for it!' 'But,' says I, 'you said you had no rooster'." The story ends right there.

Then there was the day a fun-loving local doctor came along and said, "Dinny, a rich American is up the road a piece and wants to see you."

"Wait till I put on me boots," said Dinny.

"Never mind the boots," replied the doctor. "Come along! He can't wait."

Once in the car, the doctor stepped on the gas and never stopped until they reached the town of Perth, fifty miles away. There he took Dinny, still in his bare feet, protesting but hungry, into a staid old Victorian hotel for dinner.

Dinny, Mary and Wilbert, all in their eighties, are timeless personalities of this lake region, without whom it would lose much of its local colour. When they are gone, it will never again be quite the same.

I had seen a painting of Witley Church, Surrey, which I liked very much, but I did not know anything about the artist, or where he lived. "He's an artist who lives at Willowbank," said someone. "You ought to go and write him up." So one Spring evening I did.

The charming little cottage is on a wide stretch of land on the bank of the river. There is an ever-changing view of Howe Island and the river, which is at its loveliest when the bright greens and blues are seen through the slate-grey patina of an April shower. The almost treeless marsh has at those times an unusual beauty all its own. It will not always be treeless, however, as the Scotts have planted about four hundred trees, as well as shrubs and a variety of flowers.

We enjoyed the evening spent talking to Ivan Scott and his charming English-born wife. They met during the first Great War. Both love a country life, and when Mr. Scott retired from business several years ago they decided to live in this interesting place at Willowbank, near Gananoque, where he used to live, and not many miles from Morton, where he was born. Here Mr. Scott paints, builds additions to the premises, and has constructed a trailer in which they go south for the winter. Mrs. Scott gardens and cans all sorts of fruits and vegetables. They often have picnics on the river or lakes.

On the walls were pictures of lovely places done at different seasons of the year. That of Miss Machar's glen was especially fine. There was a sketch of their only child, Judy.

Mr. Gerald A. Scott, editor and publisher of *The Gananoque Reporter* is a nephew of Ivan Scott.

That Leeds residents are broad-minded and free from bigotry is exemplified by the old gentleman who gave the land for the Methodist Church, helped build the Orange Hall, and donated fifty dollars toward the building of St. Patrick's Roman Catholic Church. He himself was an Anglican who liked to don an old brown plug hat and its accompanying regalia and take part in an Orange parade.

XI

They Return To The Land

I remember, I remember
The house where I was born,
The little window where the sun
Came peeping in at morn.

—THOMAS HOOD.

WHEN THE GRAND TRUNK RAILWAY, and later the Brockville and Westport line, passed through the county a new era of prosperity came to Leeds. The people could now find more and quicker markets for the things they made and grew. Homes were furnished with good solid furniture and more conveniences. The daughters of the house had pretty silk dresses; parties, weddings and other social events were affairs of a more sophisticated type. The mother and father still worked very hard, but the young folk were well dressed and, being full of fun and vitality, thought nothing of driving miles to a gay party and getting up after a few hours' sleep for a long day of hard work on the farm. Women aged rather more quickly than men in those days, and at sixty it was generally felt that one's life work was done. Still, few wished to move away from a large, comfortable farm home, where there was always plenty, to a more restricted life in town.

Then came a change. About the beginning of the twentieth century times were not so good. Men and women on the farms grew tired of slaving for a bare sustenance, especially those whose children had sought greener pastures in the city. Many moved into town. There they had an easier life; they made more money, and even, in some cases, began to feel somewhat patronizing toward the poorer, struggling, rather ill-dressed people who were foolish enough to remain on the farm. Hitherto, there had been a closer feeling between the people of the country and those of the town. They had had a great deal of social intercourse, and the better off families had the same advantages, the same kind of clothes. In town and country both sent their sons to college if they were at all able; many sent their daughters to college or private school. If anything, the farmer of the old stock, with a comfortable stone or brick house and many fertile acres, felt sorry for the poor town dweller who must purchase all his necessities in a store. And often his more spacious way of life was envied by the town dweller.

It was, in many cases, a rather patriarchal form of existence, copied almost unconsciously from that of the people in the land from which they came. Visit any Old

Country house of the British Isles today, and you will find many of the same customs and much of the same background and atmosphere which many in middle life can remember on a large Canadian farm. There were, of course, fewer servants, usually only a "hired girl" and one or two hired men; they were treated as human beings and often as one of the family, but nevertheless they had as much respect for the master and mistress of the domain as if they ate in a servants' hall. And a great deal more affection. Some of my happiest memories are of the grand girls who helped run the house, cleaning and cooking, milking cows, and in one instance even making over our clothes. They deserve a monument to their memory, these kindly, overworked hired girls. Of all these, I think, my favourite was a lassie "frae Glesga," who told us stories (for she was a great reader) and sang wonderful Scotch songs.

But now the wheel has come full circle, and the descendants of the early settlers are going back to the land. Grandchildren, yes, even great-grandchildren, they are returning to the land. Best of all, many who retire do so right on their own farms, or buy a little place in the country, where a man has something to do besides walking down town for the groceries or the mail. They live longer, and it's a lot more fun. In all those of pioneer blood, there is a great nostalgia for the soil.

We started out one lovely summer morning with no objective but rambling along the roads which skirt the lakes of Leeds. When we came to the Warburton road, we turned to the left and drove on to Kelsey's Corners, at Sand Bay. Turning to the right, we continued along the rocky, winding Lost Bay road. Soon we had a glorious view of Lost Bay, on whose wild, secluded shore there is

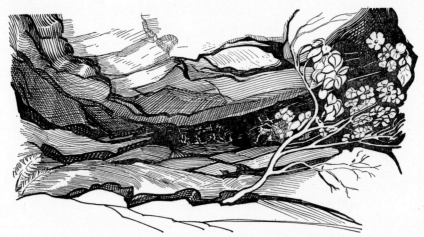

CAVES IN THE ROCK ON CHARLESTON LAKE

a splendid beach. Raspberries were growing in abundance on both sides of the road. We stopped the car and ate until we could eat no more. Then we drove down the Black Rapids road to Long Point.

"Why, what can be going on at the old O'Connor place?" I exclaimed, as we came to the weather-beaten house opposite the old stone school. The doors and windows were open. Three cars with a doctor's D on the license plates were parked at the side of the road. A burly gentleman was yanking up huge weeds out of the front lawn and hurling them over his head.

"Is anyone living here?" I called, adding, as he came nearer, "Are you Dr. Fergus O'Connor's son?"

"Yes, I'm Fergus Junior," he answered. "Here is my father now." And as he spoke our old family friend, Dr. Fergus O'Connor, of Kingston, hurried out of the door of the old homestead where he was born.

"Who is living here, Dr. O'Connor?" I asked. "You know I write about these things in my column, and I'm awfully curious, of course."

"My daughter is going to," he answered, happily. "Her husband has not been well, and when he recovered he just felt that he couldn't go on working among machines. He is an electrical engineer. They have five small children, and they want to bring them up right here. They are glad there is a school across the road. Come in and see what we are doing."

Dr. Fergus sounded quite excited. He had lost his tired appearance. His eyes were bright and sparkling, and his colour fresh and clear. It was evident that, in his joyous return to his native home, he had discovered a tonic more potent than any found in bottles. It seemed as if the place had been taken over by the whole clan who were busily cleaning up the house and grounds. Everyone was working madly, and everyone was having a grand time. Huge strips of paper swirled from the walls, plaster fell on one's head, dust flew in front of busy brooms. There were daughters-in-law, a daughter, another son, a cousin, and in the midst of them all, sweet-faced Mrs. O'Connor Senior smiled happily as she thought of the house that was again being made into a home. Already the place was wired. Nearby were a couple of oaks that would be made into floors.

"Here," said Dr. O'Connor, showing me the down-stairs bedroom, "is where I was born." We went on through all the rooms. All the woodwork was hand turned, that in the parlour being unusually well done, with panels under the sills of the windows. The floors had nice wide boards. A quaint old stair rail bordered the stairs. There was plenty of room upstairs, and the dormer window at the end of the hall was set deeply in the roof. Best of all, at the right a door opened into a huge store-room which would, I imagine, double as a playroom for the children on a rainy day.

"It's going to be a fine old home again," I said. "I am so glad the O'Connors are coming back. I guess Kathleen Roney (his cousin) will never get this door now. She said she wanted it the last time we went by."

"No, I guess she won't," he said, looking possessively at the hospitable old door.

The daughter and her husband had not yet arrived, but some other friends had come with them, and they were all having a picnic down on the shore at the miners' chimney, only a field away, when their stint of work for the day was done.

As we went out to the car, Dr. Fergus O'Connor, Junior, chanting, "I'm working off my frustrations!" was still hurling great weeds over his head.

"Truly the O'Connors have come back to their own," I said, as we drove away.

The O'Connors own another house on a nearby farm, the old miners' hotel, and Dr. Maurice O'Connor is planning to make it into a summer home. Beside it a lane leads down to a fine sandy shore.

Weeks later I drove past the old homestead. I had a special interest in it. For generations our families had been friends. My folks would stop off for dinner on the way to Lyndhurst with the grist; they would stop at my people's home on the way to Lansdowne to shop. Also, both families came from County Wexford — both Irish, which is always a tie. Already the place looked changed.

Margaret O'Connor Dougherty and her husband, Allen, were in residence. A baby's buggy was on the verandah, washing on the line. Mr. Dougherty was driving to lecture at Queen's University in Kingston every day. And in the old Long Point school, no doubt little Doughertys were learning the three R's. Then in Kingston one evening I met a relative of the O'Connor's, Dr. Leo Palmer, once written up in *The New Yorker* for his success as head of the Walkhill institution, New York. "I'm going out to the Dougherty's tomorrow," he said. "I hear they are liking it fine."

Anyway, I am sure of one thing — from now on Dr. Fergus O'Connor, Junior, will spend a great deal of his time in this lovely section of the county where he was born.

The Doughertys will not lack for neighbours. Another electrical engineer lives on the next farm. We were driving along that road one Sunday when we decided to visit the tall stone chimney down at the shore, which was used when they operated the old mine. "Stop at that house," I suggested, "and see if we can drive down the lane." My brother went over to the small frame house, whose windows looked a little different from the average in that they had some fine old pieces of pottery on the sills. When he knocked a tall, middle-aged man with clear-cut, unmistakably English features and a military bearing, came to the door. Clad in well-cut jodhpurs and a khaki shirt, he looked a more cosmopolitan type than is usually seen in those wild and rocky hills of the lakeland of Leeds. As I expected, an accent faintly reminiscent of Oxford came floating to my ears.

"I've simply got to get to the bottom of this!" I exclaimed, when my brother returned to the car. He took a dim view of such snoopiness; even being a columnist, he felt, was no excuse. So on we went down the path. We explored the 65-foot chimney, so beautifully constructed by those Englishmen of long ago. The base is now used as a fireplace for picnic parties, and all that is left of two small houses are the cellars overgrown with brush.

As we went on down to the shore a head popped up over the hill, and a voice called, "Yoo-hoo!"

"Yoo-hoo!" I answered, my journalistic nose scenting opportunity in some form.

"Oh. you're not the people I thought you were," exclaimed the voice defensively, as we came into view. This time the accent seemed Cockney.

"That's all right," I said soothingly, advancing warily lest our unsuspecting quarry take flight. "Who owns this land?"

"Mr. Mardock," he replied.

"Is he English?" I asked.

"Yes, but he has lived in Canada for some years."

"Are you going to farm?"

"Yes," he said, "we're going to farm these two farms."

Just then a dignified youngish couple hove in sight. I ventured to ask them a few questions, but they answered briefly, thinking, quite rightly, no doubt, that any female wandering about dressed in disreputable old blue jeans ought not to speak before being introduced. A bit discouraged, I clambered up the hill, just as the rest of what was evidently a jolly picnic party appeared. My relative, trying to look as if I didn't belong to him, had

gone on ahead. But fate was kind. The English gentleman now came striding down the path, and in the
friendliest manner stopped and began to chat. Carefully,
I explained that, aside from the fact that I was dying of
curiosity, I had to have material for my column. He did
not mind in the least.

"Tell me," I said, "why did you decide to settle here?"

"Well," he said, "it had all the specifications. Wood,
land, water, everything. My wife and I both hate the
city and love the country. So, after hunting all around
Ottawa and other places, we happened to find out that
this place was for sale. Bill," indicating our friend with
the Cockney accent, "is the agricultural expert."

We told him we loved that part of the country, but
that not many people wanted to live so far back, in such
an isolated place.

"The people around here," he proclaimed, "live in
paradise and don't know it."

He was born and educated in Surrey, England, as
was his wife. He had served as an officer in the Royal
Navy, and afterward they had lived in Brazil. But
nowhere that they had lived had been as beautiful as
Leeds.

All the natives of Long Point, he said, still spoke of
the "Miners' Picnic," although none could possibly
remember it unless they were more than seventy years
old. There were a thousand guests and many games and
other amusements, and plenty of refreshments for all.
That must have been just before the English company
left and the mine closed down.

I called afterward to see if Mr. and Mrs. Mardock
still liked their new home. They were happy in its

possession and not disillusioned in the least. It was Spring, and Mr. Mardock was helping with the spring's work during the weekend. But he was glad to come in and chat.

Inside, Mrs. Mardock had cleverly transformed the place, so that a little of Old England had been transplanted to the Canadian woods. There were some magnificent sixteenth century Spanish antiques, one a large writing desk with dozens of fascinating little curved drawers.

Through the week the farm is capably operated by Mrs. Mardock and the one hired man, for Mr. Mardock goes to work in the Ottawa English Electric Company from Monday until Friday night. But when Saturday comes, he is pottering happily about the farm.

"My people were of the old English yeoman stock," explained Mrs. Mardock. "Maybe that's why I love the land."

Of yeoman stock, and also with military records, were often the first settlers of Leeds. It is fine that this type of people are again coming back to the land.

The Stevens family were an early family of Leeds. Years ago they left Athens to carry on a successful business in Montreal. Now one of them has returned to the county, buying the old Purvis homestead at Mallorytown, and making a place of beauty inside and out of the more than a century-old stone house. Here, with his dogs and guns, he lives a busy and happy life, sketching and doing very creditable work in oils, and generally enjoying life. At present he is teaching an art class in Brockville, composed of amateurs who are interested in sketching, water colours and oils.

Mr. and Mrs. Arthur Hudson gave up farming when their eldest son was able to take over things, but they did not go to town. They moved into an old farmhouse about a stone's throw down from their former home. Then they renovated it, and put in all sorts of modern conveniences, so that now many city people would envy them their home. The living room, with its decor of very pale blue-green, even to the bricks in the fireplace, was a joy to the eye.

It is a good thing for the county as a whole that those who were once living in towns and cities are going back to the land. They have much of value to contribute to rural community life. The newcomer learns a great deal of solid everyday wisdom from those who are native to the place, and he is surprised that there are so many interesting community activities in which he can take part. Those who are native to the place find their outlook broadened by contact with those who have come from urban centres. Often the newcomer is astonished at the reading and thinking which the people in the country are doing. The Farm Forum and the Women's Institutes can take the credit for this. As yet, I have not found anyone in Leeds regretting that he had gone back to the land.

XII

Journey's End

SOMETIMES, WHEN I HAVE odd ingredients I would like to use, I go into my kitchen and make a cake. It has no particular name, this recipe, and I am never at all sure how it may turn out, using as I do anything I happen to have on hand. Unblushingly, I admit that that is how this book was written. Certain things were floating about in my consciousness. I collected them, and here you have the result. I had not even intended it to be this size, but this child of my brain grew out of its first meagre garments and had to have a larger covering.

I wrote *Leeds the Lovely* simply because I wanted people to realize how lovely the little known parts of our county are. Everyone knows of the beauty of the St. Lawrence and the Thousand Islands, but of the rest of this region little has been written. A great deal more might be written about this county; I write only about that which I know best, the lake district, near which I was born. One day I hope to know more about Chaffey's Locks, Portland, Westport, New Dublin and many other interesting communities. For the time being, I had to confine myself more especially to the region which I shall always think of as "The Little Killarney of Leeds."

I am essentially a countrywoman, and more than a decade of living in the New York area did not change that fact. We who come of people who, in this country and in the British Isles, have for generations owned their own land, will, I think, always feel a deep love for the soil. I do think that, if ever anyone deserved to be called "Gentle-folk," it was those of our county whom I have known who had to work at hard and often exhausting labour every day of their lives. It is easy to look like a great lady when one has servants to work for one, fine clothes and a life of comparative ease. I feel that not enough credit has been given to the women of the early part of the century, who had to work hard in large, inconvenient farmhouses all day long with children clinging to their skirts, who rose early to help milk and went out to the stable again at night, but who, when evening came, could preside at their supper tables with as much grace and charm as if they had a whole staff of servants instead of, in rare instances, a "hired girl." They were not big, lumbering women with brawny arms and broad, clumsy feet. Many of them had unusual beauty until time and labour took its toll. The man of the house, sitting in quiet dignity at the head of the table, was an impressive and unassuming host. They sent their sons and daughters to college when possible, and they themselves had often read widely — Scott, Dickens, Thackeray and the better poets. I remember an older relative telling

JOURNEY'S END

of visiting such a farm home, a lovely old stone house with a long verandah, when she was a child.

"I shall never forget Helen that evening," she said. "She came down the stairs dressed in a green velvet gown, reciting some lines of poetry as she came."

Quaint and amusing it may seem to us of this generation. Perhaps the world has lost something when a young lady in a country home today would be more likely to tear down the stairs dressed in shorts and a midriff top, shouting, "Hi, gang!" than to sweep down in a velvet gown with the words of a poem on her lips.

So I have written here and there a little about a way of life which had something spacious and solid and good about it, and which has almost disappeared. You may travel the length and breadth of Leeds, and never find a soul living on a farm who has read Scott or Jane Austen. You may even decide, as one visitor to a remote part of the county did, that we are all illiterate, and that such people as I have written about do not, and never did, exist. But they did, and they may still be found. They formed part of a background which should not be forgotten, and which had an important part in the development of Leeds.

Of course, we have all kinds of people. Some are not the kind you would come across the border to meet. Not all of us do as we would be done by, many of us have our values confused, but, on the whole, you will find there are as many fine all-wool-and-a-yard-wide folks here as anywhere else, and that it is not a bad place to live. Quite a few who have moved in from other parts seem to agree. Whether you find the people of whom I have written or not, there is one thing you will discover, one thing which remains ever the same, and that is the scenery. Leeds was lovely then. It is lovely still.